# TABLE OF CONTENTS

The *Everyday Questions* Experience ....... 
Overview of Weekly Sessions ....... 
A Message from the RZIM Team .... 11
Speaker Bios ..................... 12

Session 1: Leader Overview ....... L1-1
Session 1: Introduction .......... S1-1

Session 2: Leader Overview ....... L2-1
Session 2: Origin, Part 1 ......... S2-1

Session 3: Leader Overview ....... L3-1
Session 3: Origin, Part 2 ......... S3-1

Session 4: Leader Overview ...... L4-1
Session 4: Meaning, Part 1 ....... S4-1

Session 5: Leader Overview ..... L5-1
Session 5: Meaning, Part 2 ....... S5-1

Session 6: Leader Overview ..... L6-1
Session 6: Morality, Part 1 ....... S6-1

Session 7: Leader Overview ..... L7-1
Session 7: Morality, Part 2 ....... S7-1

Session 8: Leader Overview ..... L8-1
Session 8: Destiny, Part 1 ........ S8-1

Session 9: Leader Overview ..... L9-1
Session 9: Destiny, Part 2 ....... S9-1

Week 2 ................... N1-3
Week 3 ................... N1-5
Week 4 ................... N1-7
Week 5 ................... N1-9
Week 6 ................... N1-11
Week 7 ................... N1-13
Week 8 ................... N1-15
Week 9 ................... N1-17

Next Steps:
Additional Resources ......... N2-1
  Origin .................. N2-3
  Meaning ................. N2-5
  Morality ................ N2-7
  Destiny ................. N2-9
  Relationships ........... N2-11

## ACKNOWLEDGEMENTS:

We wish to thank Ryan Hall, Senior Pastor of Harvest Bible Chapel: Palos, and Kent Shaw, Executive Director of Harvest Bible Fellowship, for their partnership with us in developing the *Everyday Questions* curriculum. Their financial backing in filming these talks at their facilities got the project started. In addition, Ryan's innovative approach to a narrative-driven small group discussion guide was the creative spark that eventually led to the *Everyday Questions* material you are now reading.

We wish to thank Ivy Tyson for her assistance in compiling the lecture notes. We are also grateful for Danielle DuRant's careful editing of the curriculum.

We wish to thank our colleagues Ivy Tyson, Robert Repke, and Kevin Abshire for their participation and insightful feedback in a pilot group discussion of this material at RZIM's headquarters.

— *Drew McNeil and Carson Weitnauer*

# ARE YOU READY FOR THE CONVERSATION?

*Everyday Questions* is uniquely designed to facilitate your spiritual growth, confidence to initiate open-ended conversations, and passion for sharing the gospel with friends and family. As you prayerfully get ready to lead your group through this material, we want to provide you with an inside look at what to expect and how to make the most of the curriculum.

> *Before reading through the Leader's Guide, we recommend you take a moment to ask God to give you his wisdom and power for leading your group.*

# THE *EVERYDAY QUESTIONS* EXPERIENCE

Whether you are a new small group leader or an experienced facilitator, we think you will find the *Everyday Questions* experience to be unique. Let's briefly look at some of the core values and principles behind the design and structure of the material.

First, it will help you to understand that at Ravi Zacharias International Ministries (RZIM), we place a high value on answering the questioner first and foremost, rather than merely the question. What does this mean? It means:

- Most people are not formally committed to a specific worldview that can be studied in a textbook; instead, they have their own unique perspective on life and spirituality.
- The motivation for a question is as important as the question itself. We need to take into account the underlying rationale for the question if we are to provide a wise and effective answer.
- While the intellectual part of seeking God is one of the important ways that people investigate Christianity, their experiences, relationships, desires, and commitments also influence whether or not they decide to follow Christ.

---

We believe that for most of us, evangelism will look less like one conversation with a hundred people and more like a hundred conversations with one person. Therefore, throughout the curriculum we demonstrate the importance of trust, integrity, and genuine care for our family and friends. The greatest opportunities for you and your group members to share the good news can be with those who know you the best.

Therefore, in this curriculum, our speakers focus less on providing formal definitions of "atheism" or "Islam," and more on illustrating

how people from different belief systems make sense of life in light of four ultimate questions:
- Origin (Where do I come from?)
- Meaning (Why do I have significance?)
- Morality (How do I differentiate right from wrong?)
- Destiny (What happens after death?)

To complement the talks, we developed a narrative experience to facilitate your group's interaction with the material. These narratives show how the topics discussed by the RZIM speaking team can be part of everyday conversations. They feature characters with a wide range of spiritual interest, from hostile to curious to very open. As you read the stories, your group will see what evangelism might look like in the context of family, friends, school, and work. Some reveal the importance of past experiences with Christians. Many of them raise questions about our emotional experience of discussing Christ with others. Each one aims to foster an attitude of compassion and empathy for the challenges and concerns of friends and neighbors, whether they follow Christ or not.

> **We believe that for most of us, evangelism will look less like one conversation with a hundred people and more like a hundred conversations with one person.**

By emphasizing the importance of responding to the individual, the approach to evangelism presented in this study does not leave room for scripted or systematic approaches. In fact, one of the main principles we want to teach through this curriculum is that in today's world, scripts are unlikely to be effective. Life and people are too complex for anyone to memorize a series of good answers to a set of expected questions. Each week's dialogue seeks to showcase the mystery, the messiness, and the multifaceted nature of real friendship and honest conversation.

As the group leader, you'll have the opportunity to adjust the details of any story to make it more relevant to your group if needed. The goal is for your group to prayerfully, empathetically, and thoughtfully consider the people and topics that are raised in each week's discussion. We are teaching a respectful and effective approach more than a set of right answers. It may help to think of the narrative like a movie that you can pause and ask, "What would you do in this situation?"

We know that each of these scenarios could have gone in many different directions. As a group, we hope that you find even better ways to ask questions, explain the gospel, and build trust with your friends than how we present Jonathan and Erica's story. Their example is not intended to be viewed as the "right" or "best" approach to these situations. We simply hope that this approach will offer a useful starting point for considering new ways of talking with loved ones about the gospel.

In one of our pilot groups, most of the group members were already having evangelistic conversations with their family and friends. This material encouraged them that everyday interactions—from conversations at work to family gatherings to discussions about how to raise kids—can naturally and comfortably include intentional, genuine ways to discuss Jesus and the good news. Each week's study provided new questions, new insights into the complexities of discussing spiritual matters, and encouragement to continue inviting family and friends into a relationship with God.

## THE IMPORTANCE OF COMMUNITY

In many ways, the group dynamics of your weekly meetings are as important for the overall *Everyday Questions* experience as the recorded talks and the participant discussion guide. Are people interacting with respect and kindness? Is there an *us vs. them* mentality towards non-Christians? Are people demonstrating empathy towards the characters in the story? What is the emotional tone of your group's conversation?

As you facilitate an accepting and open environment for discussion, you will be modeling the very relational qualities that *Everyday Questions* aims to teach. Ultimately, we hope this is how your group members will treat their friends who are not Christians.

As you prepare for this curriculum, think about how you want to bring your group together. Your pastor or other leaders may recommend other great ideas for building community in your small group. Most importantly, remember that as a leader, your actions and lifestyle set the tone for the other members of your group.
Ideas for building community in your group:
- Pray for each member of your group.
- Be intentional about building personal relationships with group members.
- Host social events outside of the scheduled group meetings.
- Remember what group members share about their lives and follow up with them about those issues.
- Be the first to experiment, take risks, and apply what you learn from *Everyday Questions*.
- If your members don't know each other well, ask some comfortable "icebreaker" questions to start out your initial meetings. For instance, "How did you hear about the group and decide to

join?" or "Share a high and low point from the last week." It helps if you go first; you can model a genuine and appropriate openness for others to imitate.

- Encourage your group to pray for each other every day. Some group leaders pass out note cards for everyone to write a few prayer requests on and then these are passed around, so that everyone is praying for another member each week. Or, you might want to create a group text message to keep everyone connected between meetings.

Overall, as the group leader, **we encourage you to create a safe environment for people to ask questions, share their experiences, and take risks to open up new conversations with those they know and love.**

Remember that the priority is your heartfelt desire to prepare, to lead well, and to care for each member of your group. In this setting, integrity, diligence, and love are far more important than doing an "excellent" job.

May God richly bless you and encourage you as you lead your *Everyday Questions* group.

---

## OVERVIEW OF THE WEEKLY SESSIONS:

Your Leader's Guide contains the same material as the Participant's Guide. In addition, your version of the workbook contains this introductory overview, a brief synopsis of the main points for each week's material, and some "quick tips" provided within the weekly discussion notes.

In general, after the first week, be sure to start your meetings by bringing up the weekly challenge from the previous meeting. Ask group members to share about any evangelistic conversations they have had since you last met. Ask for updates on any prayer requests or personal issues they have shared.

Also, if people join your group after you get started, or arrive late, you may need to remind them of the main characters in the story:

- The stories feature Jonathan and Erica and their children Trevor and Alyssa.
- After Erica came to faith in Christ, Jonathan started to investigate and eventually became a believer as well.
- While Trevor is questioning his faith, and Alyssa's spiritual perspective is unclear throughout the story, they are both watching and learning from how their parents live out their beliefs and discuss the gospel with others.

Some members of your group may ask about the video guide. The video guides are intended to make it easier for participants to follow along with the videos. These notes include excerpts for the main points made by the speaking team, the biblical references, and many of the quotes. If anyone asks you, the video guide are not intended to be a replacement for watching the lectures nor are they a word-for-word transcript of everything that the speaker shares. The idea is that your group members will not need to write down all of these points for themselves.

> **We encourage you to create a safe environment for people to ask questions, share their experiences, and take risks to open up new conversations with those they know and love.**

After watching the video each week, we encourage you to pause and ensure that there is shared understanding of the material covered.

While you probably won't have the time to discuss every question that group members may have from the lecture, it is important for everyone to feel like they understand at least the main point of the talk before moving into the discussion guide. Depending on how much time you have, you might ask, "What was the main point of the lecture?" or "Were there any points you found confusing or unclear?"

By opening up space for discussion and even disagreement about the talk, you can model the values of the curriculum. At the same time, because this material invites so much open-ended conversation, you may want to push past an extended discussion of the talk. Also, sometimes the questions that group members have from the lecture are naturally answered during the small group discussion.

Every group is different when it comes to the discussion section. Some groups are filled with vocal, energetic participants. Others are quieter and prioritize listening carefully to one another. Sometimes just one person tries to do all of the talking! Whatever the particular nature of your group, it is likely that you will need to keep one eye on the clock. The "discuss together" questions are usually very open-ended, so any number of them could lead into extended conversations.

The better you know your group, the easier it may become to select which questions to spend more time on and which questions to spend less time on or skip altogether. By reading through the participant discussion in advance of each week's discussion, you can prayerfully decide which topics or themes you want to focus on. Of course, you can always change your approach once you see which issues seem to be the most interesting and relevant for your group. It may be less important to complete each week's discussion than to have a really good conversation about just one or two questions.

❗ **You can always change your approach once you see which issues seem to be the most interesting and relevant for your group. It may be less important to complete each week's discussion than to have a really good conversation about just one or two questions.**

While this material is written for a general audience, what matters now that it is in your hands is the particular people in your group. What could be a diversion for one group is possibly the most important point for your community. If your situation allows for it, you may want to extend the discussion of some scenarios for an additional week. At other times, you will need to interrupt even really energetic conversations in order to move the group along to the next section of the narrative. Whatever decision you make, remember that the primary goal is to encourage each participant to be faithful, wise, and respectful in sharing the gospel.

👤 *Finally, we encourage you to take the pressure off yourself. Trust God to be at work in your own life and in the lives of those who participate. This is our prayer for you as you lead your small group through this material:*

**"I thank my God in all my remembrance of you, always in every prayer of mine for you all making my prayer with joy, because of your partnership in the gospel from the first day until now. And I am sure of this, that he who began a good work in you will bring it to completion at the day of Jesus Christ."**

—Philippians 1:3-6

But in your hearts honor Christ the Lord as holy, always being prepared to make a defense to anyone who asks you for a reason for the hope that is in you; yet do it with gentleness and respect, having a good conscience, so that, when you are slandered, those who revile your good behavior in Christ may be put to shame.

—*1 Peter 3:15-16, ESV*

## A MESSAGE FROM THE RZIM TEAM

We probably all know that as Christians we are called to share our faith. The question is whether or not it actually happens. If it doesn't, there may be any number of reasons as to why. It could be a lack of confidence to explain the gospel. It could be fear of what questions we might be asked. It could also be that where you live, being a Christian invites ridicule or even hostility. Whatever the reason for not sharing our faith, many of us have seen family members and friends drift away from God or from the church.

*Everyday Questions* is designed to make it easier for all of us to engage with the people around us. Regardless of how you feel right now about evangelism, our goal is to make it comfortable for you to have great conversations with your family, friends, neighbors, and co-workers about the most important issues in life.

We called this study *Everyday Questions* because the topics addressed in this study really do appear in our daily lives. It takes some skill to begin to recognize them in their various forms, but the reality is that we all will have opportunities to discuss the big questions about life with the people we care about and see every day.

In each week's session, the RZIM team will both clarify the central beliefs of Christianity and explain how to share them in a persuasive and gracious way. The group discussions should give you some ideas about how to talk about those beliefs comfortably with family, friends, and co-workers. The goal isn't to become an expert or to have all the answers, but to be thoughtful, respectful, and sincere in discussing meaningful questions with those you know and love.

We're praying for God to work powerfully in your lives!

*Sincerely yours,*
**Drew McNeil**
**Carson Weitnauer**
Ravi Zacharias International Ministries

## SPEAKER BIOS

### *Ravi Zacharias*

Ravi Zacharias is a noted author and speaker who has been invited to present the claims of the Judeo-Christian worldview on university campuses, in halls of government, and numerous forums around the world for 44 years. He has addressed writers of the peace accord in South Africa, the president's cabinet and parliament in Peru, military officers at the Lenin Military Academy and  the Center for Geopolitical Strategy in Moscow as well as students at Oxford, Cambridge, Harvard, Johns Hopkins, and elsewhere.

Dr. Zacharias has twice spoken at the Annual Prayer Breakfast at the United Nations, which marks the opening day of the UN General Assembly, and has also addressed National Prayer Breakfasts at the seats of government in Ottawa, Canada, and London, England. As the 2008 Honorary Chairman of the National Day of Prayer, he gave addresses at the White House, the Pentagon, and The Cannon House.

He is the author of more than twenty books spanning the fields of theology, apologetics, comparative religions, and philosophy. For his lifetime of work, Dr. Zacharias has been conferred with seven honorary doctorates, most recently a Doctor of Public Service and a Doctor of Laws (2016). He hosts the international radio programs *Let My People Think* and *Just Thinking* and is Founder and President of Ravi Zacharias International Ministries.

## Andy Bannister

Andy is the Director of the Solas Centre for Public Christianity and an Adjunct Speaker for Ravi Zacharias International Ministries, speaking and teaching regularly throughout the UK, Europe, Canada, the USA, and the wider world. From universities to churches, business forums to TV and radio, Andy regularly address audiences of both Christians and those of all faiths and none on issues relating to faith, culture, politics and society.

Andy holds a PhD in Islamic studies and has taught extensively at universities across Canada, the USA, the UK and further afield on both Islam and philosophy. Andy is also an Adjunct Research Fellow at the Centre for the Study of Islam and Other Faiths at Melbourne School of Theology.

Andy is the author of *An Oral-Formulaic Study of the Qur'an* and *Heroes: Five Lessons From Whose Lives We Can Learn*. His latest book, *The Atheist Who Didn't Exist (or: The Dreadful Consequences of Really Bad Arguments)*, is a humorous engagement with the New Atheism. Andy also co-wrote and presented the TV documentary *Burning Questions*.

When not travelling, speaking, or writing, Andy is a keen hiker, mountain climber and photographer. He is married to Astrid and they have two children, Caitriona and Christopher.

## *Stuart McAllister*

Born in Scotland, Stuart McAllister saw his life changed by Christ at the early age of twenty. Filled with a hunger to learn more and deepen his understanding of the faith led him to join Operation Mobilization in 1978. He worked with the organization for twenty years in Vienna, Austria, and his service took him to Yugoslavia, where he was imprisoned for forty days for distributing Christian literature. Upon his release, he continued to work in communist countries, resulting in more imprisonments.

With a rich history of service, Stuart has acted as general secretary of the European Evangelical Alliance (1992-1998) and been involved with the European Lausanne Committee. He developed a mobilization movement called "Love Europe," which sent several thousand team members across Europe with the message of the Christian faith. Stuart also founded the European Roundtable, bringing together a diverse group of ministries and interests that collaborated to foster "Hope for Europe."

Stuart joined Ravi Zacharias International Ministries in 1998 as the International Director and today serves as Global Support Specialist. With a heavy travel schedule that takes him all over the globe, Stuart speaks in churches, universities, and other forums with the same passion he first knew as a follower of Christ. Stuart has been a lecturer at Alliance Theological Seminary in Nyack, New York, where he was honored with a Doctor of Divinity. Additionally, he has been a featured speaker several times at the European Leadership Forum.

Stuart is a frequent contributor to *A Slice of Infinity*, RZIM's daily reading on issues of apologetics and philosophy, *Just Thinking*, the ministry's quarterly journal, as well as *Engage*, a magazine published quarterly by RZIM Educational Trust. He has also contributed chapters in the books *Beyond Opinion* (Thomas Nelson, 2007) and *Global Missiology for the 21st Century* (World Evangelical Fellowship, 2000).

### *Abdu Murray*

Abdu Murray is North American Director with Ravi Zacharias International Ministries and is the author of two books, including his latest, *Grand Central Question: Answering the Critical Concerns of the Major Worldviews*. For most of his life, Abdu was a proud Muslim who studied the Qur'an and Islam. After a nine year investigation into the historical, philosophical, and scientific underpinnings of the major world religions and views, Abdu discovered that the historic Christian faith can answer the questions of the mind and the longings of the heart.

Abdu has spoken to diverse international audiences and has participated in debates and dialogues across the globe. He has appeared as a guest on numerous radio and television programs all over the world.

Abdu holds a BA in Psychology from the University of Michigan and earned his *Juris Doctor* from the University of Michigan Law School. As an attorney, Abdu was named several times in *Best Lawyers in America* and *Michigan Super Lawyer*. Abdu is the Scholar in Residence of Christian Thought and Apologetics at the Josh McDowell Institute of Oklahoma Wesleyan University.

Abdu lives in the Detroit area with his wife and their three children.

## John Njoroge

John is a member of the speaking team at Ravi Zacharias International Ministries. He speaks frequently on university campuses, churches, and conferences around the world. His passion is to help clear the fog between the academy and the local church by making the case for the credibility of the gospel of Jesus Christ in a winsome and persuasive manner.

He is a summa cum laude graduate of Talbot School of Theology where he earned a master's degree in philosophy, a master's degree in New Testament studies, and a master of theology. While at Talbot, he also served as a graduate teaching assistant and an adjunct faculty member.

John is the host of the African versions of RZIM's radio programs *Let My People Think* and *Just Thinking*, which are heard in several countries across the African continent. He is in the process of completing a PhD in philosophy at the University of Georgia. He lives in Kenya with his wife, Leah, and their two boys, Jonathan and Benjamin.

## *Michael Ramsden*

Michael Ramsden is the International Director of RZIM and has been part of RZIM since its foundation in Europe in 1997. Michael is also joint Director of the Oxford Centre for Christian Apologetics. Michael was brought up in the Middle East and later moved to England where he worked for the Lord Chancellor's department investing funds.

While doing research in Law and Economics at Sheffield University, he taught Moral Philosophy and lectured for the International Seminar for Jurisprudence and Human Rights in Strasbourg. He has also been a Professor-in-Residence at the Wolfsberg Executive Institute in Switzerland. Michael has been invited to lecture in various settings including the White House in Washington DC and has in the past addressed leaders at NATO HQ in Brussels, Members of the European Parliament, as well as bankers and investment managers on the current global financial crisis. Michael is also involved in a number of initiatives to equip and train emerging leaders and evangelists around the world. Michael lives in Oxford with his wife, Anne, and their three children.

## LEADER OVERVIEW FOR SESSION 1:

From the start of the curriculum, we encourage you to engage your group and begin the dialogue! Session 1 intentionally begins with a question—What comes to mind when you hear the phrase "share your faith"?—that you can use to begin your group's conversation about evangelism.

If your group isn't familiar with RZIM, you might want to email them links to our website (www.rzim.org) and our YouTube page (https://www.youtube.com/user/rzimmedia).

After reading through the "Introduction" session, you might want to invite your group to share how comfortable they feel engaging in more open dialogue about questions, doubts, and even disagreements with others.

> **As the leader, take responsibility for leading your small group to be a safe and accepting environment for everyone to discover new insights about God and his Word.**

Some might be very comfortable with debate, but need to reconsider how they can develop the ability to listen well, find common ground, and give space for more reserved members to participate. You'll need to determine whether your group needs more encouragement to openly discuss their doubts or, by contrast, to become increasingly gentle, kind, and respectful in the midst of regular disagreement. As the leader, take responsibility for leading your small group to be a safe and accepting environment for everyone to discover new insights about God and his Word.

Though we briefly reference Jonathan and Erica in this week's session, your group will meet them in next week's session. If anyone is curious and wants to know more, let them know this is just a bit of foreshadowing.

For the additional study materials, since not everyone will have the time for this material, we've placed it at the end where those who are interested can go deeper. As the leader, we encourage you to read through the additional study sections. This will enable you to point group members to this section whenever it might be helpful for them.

Some members of your group may be interested in doing the provided Bible study. This is a great way to deepen your understanding of the materials covered in each week's lesson, but this is not homework or required reading for the upcoming lesson. We simply want to encourage all participants to stay grounded in God's Word so we have provided these short devotional guides for each week. You may want to consult with your pastor about a recommended study Bible that group members can use to find additional information on these passages of Scripture. Rather than giving your group pre-packaged answers about what the Bible says, our goal is to encourage each participant to develop the habit of reading the Bible, asking good questions about what it means, and to become comfortable finding answers as they study the Scriptures.

*For your first week together, especially if you are leading a new group, it is usually best for the leader to pray. If you don't know someone well, be sure to ask their permission before you ask them to lead the group in prayer. Not everyone feels comfortable doing this.*

## Notes for Small Group Interaction

**1-1.** Some people may mention well-known, public evangelists like Billy Graham. The aim of this question is to get us to identify and learn from the example of less known evangelists. Perhaps your parents, a friend in college, a pastor, or someone you know at church. Few of us can emulate someone like Billy Graham, but the people we respect from our own context can teach us a great deal about how to be an attractive witness for Christ.

**1-2.** The aim of this question is primarily to find out what experience and general feelings your group has concerning evangelism. It may be that some strong feelings come out towards other approaches in this conversation, but the aim is not to critique other methods, merely to share with one another what your starting point is for this study.

**1-3.** This is a challenging question! The point here is that, as a matter of integrity and authenticity, we are inviting the group to be open about areas where they feel they need to grow and to hopefully create a safe environment for people to share honestly whether or not their lives are currently causing others to ask them questions.

"I thank my God in all my remembrance of you, always in every prayer of mine for you all making my prayer with joy, because of your partnership in the gospel from the first day until now. And I am sure of this, that he who began a good work in you will bring it to completion at the day of Jesus Christ."
—*Philippians 1:3-6*

# Session 1: Introduction

What comes to mind when you hear the phrase "share your faith"?

Many of us feel intimidated or discouraged. Others are motivated and enthusiastic. Or you may be somewhere in between. But by the end of this study, we hope you feel excited by the opportunity to have meaningful conversations about what matters most in life.

Regardless of where you are today, the reality of who God is and his purposes for the world are of the greatest importance. God isn't just a part of life; he has defined and created all of life. There is no issue or experience that is not connected to God in some way. We were created to know God, and all of life is best understood in light of that truth. *Everyday Questions* will address how we can learn to discuss him with people around us in a mature, thoughtful, and relevant manner.

Each week, you will watch a video featuring an RZIM speaker. Our speakers engage audiences around the world with clear, thoughtful presentations of the gospel and its relevance to life. The message will give you new ideas for how you can effectively discuss your faith. To make it easy to follow along, notes are provided for each talk.

After the video concludes, your group will discuss the message. The goal is not to perfectly answer every question. Rather, the purpose is to learn how to talk about God in a way that feels comfortable, interesting, and enjoyable, even (and especially) when you believe different things. We encourage you to help your group be a safe place for questions, doubts, and even disagreement. Sharing the gospel requires that we make every effort to show respect and empathy to every person.

These sessions cover the four basic worldview topics:
1. Origin (Where do I come from?)
2. Meaning (Why do I have significance?)
3. Morality (How do I differentiate right from wrong?)
4. Destiny (What happens after death?)

A worldview is like a pair of glasses: it is the basic set of assumptions that shape how we see the world around us. A deep understanding of these four issues will prepare us to discuss significant matters with nearly anyone that we meet.

Each week, we've built the discussion section around a story about Jonathan and Erica. As you read about them, we want you to try to put yourself in their shoes. Apply their circumstances to your own life where possible. We recognize there are many family and life circumstances that are different from Jonathan and Erica's. Feel free to adapt the details so they better address your own situation. Together, we want you to have the opportunity to try out new ways of asking questions and having great conversations about God. Throughout the narrative, we assume that Jonathan and Erica are familiar with the main points provided by the RZIM speaking team. We hope their integration of these ideas into daily conversations will inspire your own approach to making this material relevant and useful.

This study won't give you an exhaustive list of answers to spiritual questions, provide a "one size fits all" method of sharing your faith, or present a philosophy or theology course. But it will allow you to hear from world-class speakers who share the gospel in a persuasive way. Their teaching will enable you to better understand and explain the Christian worldview. You will become more familiar with other worldviews and become more empathetic in understanding other people's point of view. You will be able to practice and discuss how to have meaningful spiritual conversations with people from different belief systems and personalities.

At the end of each session, we encourage you to share about your family and friends. Pray for one another. Pray for God to open doors for conversations about the gospel.

If you want to do further study on the topics covered, we've provided some additional resources for you at the end of the workbook.
This study will stretch you and train you to talk with many types of people who need to hear of God's love. We hope it is a gentle and positive stretching of your comfort zone, so that by the end of the study, you will feel far more prepared to talk with others about Christ.

To get started, please enjoy a brief welcome video from Ravi Zacharias. *Before starting the video, we encourage a member of your group to start the time with a prayer.*

# Video Guide

This video guide is intended to make it easy for you to take notes on Ravi's message. The main ideas and quotes are listed below for your convenience.

# An Introduction to *Everyday Questions*

Questions are a vital part of our lives.

As we mature, we are building our worldview. A worldview pulls together the answers to four fundamental questions:
- The question of origin
- The question of meaning
- The question of morality
- The question of destiny

*Everyday Questions* will help you put together a coherent set of meaningful answers.

Apologetics deals with two fundamental issues.

1. Giving answers to the questions people ask

*"But in your hearts honor Christ the Lord as holy, always being prepared to make a defense to anyone who asks you for a reason for the hope that is in you; yet do it with gentleness and respect."* (1 Peter 3:15-16)

2. Clarifying truth claims (Peter in Acts 2)

The goal is not to defeat the questioner but to win the questioner. The ultimate victory comes when the Holy Spirit changes their hearts towards him, but you and I are the means and the instruments of answering questions and clarifying truth claims.

> *Before going to the small group interaction, you may want to pause and make sure everyone feels comfortable with at least the main points of the lecture.*

## Small Group Interaction

Ravi Zacharias has maintained an effective evangelistic presence for over forty years to the world's leaders in the context of the academy, the arts, businesses, churches, and government. His influence has grown through personal interactions, public speaking, radio and internet broadcasts, and books. At the heart of his message to us is the idea that, "The gospel is true and beautiful. It has to be presented in a winsome way."

1. Who are some of your personal role models in evangelism? Who do you know that lives out their convictions and expresses their faith in an attractive manner? What do they do—and what do they avoid doing—that makes them role models?

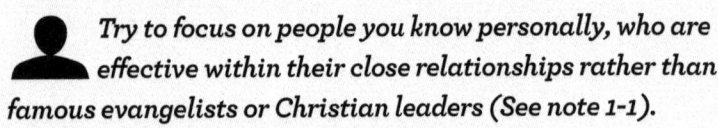

*Try to focus on people you know personally, who are effective within their close relationships rather than famous evangelists or Christian leaders (See note 1-1).*

2. Have you gone through evangelism training before? What was the method, and how did it go? What hesitations or concerns do you have about this course?

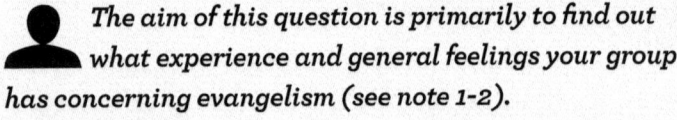

*The aim of this question is primarily to find out what experience and general feelings your group has concerning evangelism (see note 1-2).*

Ravi builds his opening introduction to us on the message of 1 Peter 3:15-16.

*"But in your hearts honor Christ the Lord as holy, always being prepared to make a defense to anyone who asks you for a reason for the hope that is in you; yet do it with gentleness and respect."*

3. This passage starts with an emphasis on "honoring Christ the Lord as holy." Peter's argument is that our heartfelt dedication to Christ will result in people asking us why we live the way we live. When was the last time someone asked you about your faith?

What do people see in your life that makes them curious enough to ask about your Christian convictions?

> *Be sensitive to any potential feelings of embarrassment or guilt in your group. Encourage your group that this study will help everyone make progress as an evangelist (see note 1-3).*

4. If we want others to share our hope in God, we need to give them a reasonable explanation of what we believe. Ravi suggests that one helpful way to approach this opportunity is by using the four building blocks of any worldview: origin, meaning, morality, and destiny. For the next eight weeks, we will gain important insights in each of these areas.

As we begin our study, how would you explain the Christian perspective on these issues?

*Origin:*

*Meaning:*

*Morality:*

*Destiny:*

> *The priority here is to see how comfortable and informed the members of your group are in regard to these pivotal issues.*

5. The final requirement for evangelism in this passage is to maintain an attitude of "gentleness and respect." We also need to keep "a good conscience." Ravi emphasized that "the goal is not to defeat the questioner, but to win the questioner."

What are some open-ended questions you could ask a friend about their spiritual beliefs?

> *Some possibilities: What do you think about God? What do you think our purpose in life is? How do you know if you're happy? Do you wish your life was different than it is?*

Discuss how these questions could demonstrate gentleness and respect.

Share from your own experience why gentleness and respect are so important:

6. Throughout this study, we want to focus on people more than ideas. Use the rest of your time to discuss your own feelings about evangelism. Discuss the good and bad experiences you have had in sharing your faith. Finally, tell the group about your family and friends who you want to know the hope and love of God.

> *The answers to this question will give you a good idea of how group members feel about evangelism. Are they enthusiastic? Prayerful? Habitually talking to their friends about Jesus? Scared? Discouraged? Resistant? Whatever the answers are, communicate your acceptance, support, and belief that God will continue to develop everyone as an evangelist over the course of your time together.*

*In next week's session, Dr. Andy Bannister, an adjunct speaker with Ravi Zacharias International Ministries, will introduce us to some new insights on the topic of origins.*

## Everyday Questions:

As a group, brainstorm some of the "everyday questions" you have heard or might hear on the topic of origins. It is rare, for most of us, to have someone formally state an academic interest in human origins. Nevertheless, the topic comes up all the time in other ways. Maybe you know someone with an interest in their family genealogy. Perhaps you have noticed references to this question in popular movies or music. Discuss together some of the everyday questions that might naturally lead into a conversation on this topic.

## Your Notes:

_____

_____

## Closing Prayer

Ravi reminded us that "The ultimate victory comes when the Holy Spirit changes their hearts towards Him, but you and I are the means and the instruments of answering questions and clarifying truth claims." Invite the Holy Spirit to give you wisdom and courage to take responsibility for sharing the gospel and to change the hearts of those you know and love.

1. Pray for one another. Pray for any needs in your life.

2. Pray for the family and friends whose names were mentioned in your earlier discussion.

> 👤 Be aware that everyone may not be comfortable praying out loud. You may want to close your first meeting in prayer or specifically ask someone you are confident is comfortable with praying for the group.

## Weekly Challenge:

This week, start some friendly conversations using a few of the open-ended questions you or your group liked the most. Afterwards, write down what you learned. Next week there will be an opportunity to share about these discussions.

> 👤 We learn new skills best when we attempt to apply them. It may be easier to focus on learning information and building good relationships with one another, but your group's commitment to taking new actions and developing new habits is an essential component of making this curriculum work.
>
> Therefore, we suggest you let your group know that you are taking the weekly challenge seriously and encourage them to do the same. Also emphasize that we're just asking them to try to start a conversation. That's it. No pressure to share the gospel or even certain ideas. It can be as simple as just asking someone a question and letting the conversation progress naturally. Hopefully that will help make it comfortable and enjoyable.

# For Further Study

If you would like to do additional study on the biblical basis for this week's session, please see the "Next Steps" section at the end of your handbook.

## LEADER OVERVIEW FOR SESSION 2:

As your group gathers for your second meeting, remember the weekly challenge from your first meeting. Share your own experience of starting new conversations and ask your group about their experiences. Continue building an accepting, encouraging environment. You want everyone to feel that it is as valuable to discuss mistakes and lessons learned as it is to celebrate good decisions and positive outcomes.

If anyone says they forgot about the challenge, be sure to thank them for their openness. Just by asking about the weekly challenge, you are encouraging your group to be intentional about applying what they are learning in the small group.

This week's curriculum is built around two important ideas:
- First, the central point of Andy's lecture is that humans are made in God's image. Therefore, all humans are equally valuable.
- Second, the primary point of the narrative is to highlight a conversational approach that is likely to build trust and open up conversations. It encourages asking questions, listening well, and looking for common ground.

After watching Andy's lecture, we encourage you to ask the group two questions before moving into the small group interaction:
- What did you think of the lecture?
- What was the main idea of Andy's presentation?

Be sure that everyone understands the main teaching point: because humans are made in God's image, we are all equally valuable.

After this first video, some participants may express fear that "I could never do that!" If this concern comes up, be prepared to offer some encouragement. The small group interaction focuses on applying the big ideas from the RZIM lectures in a personal and appropriate way. Together, everyone in your group can make progress.

**❗ Be sure that everyone understands the main teaching point: because humans are made in God's image, we are all equally valuable.**

The small group interaction focuses on a family conversation around the dinner table. The focus of this curriculum is not on parenting, but an approach to conversations about faith that can work in nearly any situation. If your group gets sidetracked into various parenting philosophies, work to bring people back to a discussion of the primary purpose of this evangelism training curriculum.

Remind your group that each week's session is built around the story with Jonathan and Erica and their children Trevor and Alyssa. From the beginning, it is important to demonstrate an interest in each character and their experiences. If you are leading a group of, say, unmarried college students, consider how you might change the characters in the story to make it more familiar, without changing the intent of the dialogue or discussion questions.

Depending on your group's life experiences, various "back stories" for Trevor and his family may be imagined. Has Trevor heard the gospel before? What kind of church does the family attend? These discussions are worthwhile as long as they can help the group better understand a key principle: the questions we ask and the approach we take will vary based upon who we are talking to.

While the narrative offers one good approach to respectfully connecting with Trevor, your group may develop a number of other helpful ways to engage in this conversation. This is a terrific outcome! We want your group to go beyond knowing more information to being prepared to build trust and open up conversations about faith with a wide variety of people. In this conversation, the parents model respect, emotional maturity, asking questions, and a long term approach.

Whenever the discussion is getting too far removed from the primary teaching points of the lecture and the narrative, we recommend that you ask a member of your group to read through the next part of the story.

# Session 2: Origin

*Origin, Part 1:*
Andy Bannister

## INTRODUCTION

> Origin: Where did everything come from?
> Meaning: Why are we here?
> Morality: What is right and wrong?
> Destiny: What happens when we die?

Jonathan and Erica have been married for seventeen years. They have two children: Trevor (15) and Alyssa (10). Jonathan has worked for the same company for nearly 20 years, and has slowly worked his way through a variety of positions there. In his current role, he is responsible for managing one of the company's departments. Erica recently began working for a local non-profit organization but has always been very active in the community. After Alyssa was born, Erica started attending a local church, where she eventually got baptized and became a member. Jonathan would occasionally go along to services with his family. Over time he became increasingly curious, and about five years ago, it all started to make sense. He realized that God had been pursuing him as well, and put his trust in Christ.

As Jonathan and Erica have both become more grounded in their own faith, the desire to share about Jesus with others has begun to increase. Together, they are starting to see that there are opportunities all around them.

*For the rest of this curriculum, we encourage you to identify with either Jonathan or Erica. The story will generally refer to them as either "you" or "your spouse" to make this a more natural and seamless experience.*

In particular, your teenage son, Trevor, comes to church with the family each week, but lately he's been less enthusiastic about going to services and his youth group. As he enters into tenth grade, he's becoming increasingly independent. And while you are happy that he takes his studies seriously, other parents have told you that Trevor's science teacher is openly critical of religion.

At the dinner table one night, as usual, you ask Trevor what he is learning about in his classes. Trevor says, "We are learning about the beginning of the universe in class. Not the fairy tale version with talking snakes."

You feel at a loss how to respond.

You know this could be a really important conversation with your son, but you're not sure you're ready to defend your views. After all, it's been a few years since you were in a science class. As his condescending comment lingers in the air, you realize you aren't sure where to start.

Trevor looks down at his plate and says, "Didn't mean to make fun of your church thing. People can believe whatever they want."

You know you need to try. So you pause for a moment to choose your words carefully.

But what do you say?

This week's video will help us talk to people about the question of our origins. As you watch, notice Andy Bannister's approach to the topic. He doesn't talk about the age of the earth, the physics of the big bang, or the formation of early molecules. Instead, he first demonstrates that he has carefully listened to what prominent atheist thinkers have to say. He spends a significant amount of time presenting and challenging their perspective on human origins. Then he starts to explain the Christian message that we are made in God's image. He shows how this truth makes sense of the human experience of hope, purpose, meaning, value, morality, and dignity. His balanced, lively approach provides us with an invaluable template for our own conversations.

*Before starting the video, have a member of your group open your time together in prayer.*

# Video Guide

This guide is intended to make it easy to take notes on Andy's message. The main ideas and quotes are outlined below for your convenience.

## The Importance of Hope

### The Question of Origins: Why Does It Matter?

*If people have real, genuine, objective hope, then we can live meaningfully. But if life is hopeless and we have no certainty for the future, then we have a problem.*

*Is there hope to be found?*

### The 4 basic worldview questions:
    1. The Question of Origins
    2. The Question of Meaning
    3. The Question of Morality
    4. The Question of Destiny

*Does life have a purpose (telos)?*

### Viktor E. Frankl
    "Ever more people today have the means to live, but no meaning to live for."

*What does it actually mean to be human?*

# An Atheist Perspective on Origins

*If you believe that there is no God--that everything is time plus chance plus natural selection—then you have to answer the question of origins and human purpose purely in terms of the material. All that matters is matter.*

## Stephen Jay Gould [1]

"We cannot read the meaning of life passively in the facts of nature. We must construct these answers ourselves — from our own wisdom and ethical sense. There is no other way."

*Can we construct our own meaning?*

- *The problem of conflicting meanings*
- *The problem of irrelevance: our personal meanings don't change the outcome*

*Are we just biology?*

## Richard Dawkins [2]

"We animals exist for their preservation and are nothing more than their [our genes] throwaway survival machines."

*Ideas have consequences.*

*If you genuinely believe that human beings are just matter, it would lead you to conclude there is no such thing as dignity and there is certainly no such thing as hope.*

---

[1] Stephen Jay Gould, as quoted in *The Meaning Of Life: Reflections In Words and Pictures On Why We Are Here*, ed. David Friend and the Editors of Life (Boston: Little, Brown, 1991), 33.
[2] Richard Dawkins, *The Selfish Gene* (Oxford: Oxford University Press, 2006), xxi.

# A Christian Perspective on Origins

### Genesis 1:26-27

*What does it mean to be human?*

### 3 foundational truths in Genesis 1:26-27:
1. Foundation for Human Value
2. Foundation for Human Dignity
3. Foundation for Ethics

## Foundation for Human Value

*How do you value a human life?*

*There is only one place where you can locate your identity and your self-worth that will actually support you—and that is in the image of God.*

### G.K. Chesterton [3]
> For religion all men are equal, as all pennies are equal, because the only value in any of them is that they bear the image of the King.

*If there is a God who has revealed himself in Jesus Christ, who has on the cross paid the ultimate price for each one of us, then each of us bears tremendous value.*

*But if atheism is true, then we bear none at all.*

---

[3] G. K. Chesteron, *Charles Dickens: A Critical Study* (New York: Dodd, Mead & Co., 1929).

**Summary**

- The question of origins directly affects how we answer the question, "What does it mean to be human?"
- The atheistic explanation of origins generates significant problems.
- The biblical foundation of human origins is first found in Genesis 1:26-27, which establishes that humans are made in the image of God.
- Because we bear God's image, we can reasonably establish that all human beings are valuable.

> *Before going to the small group interaction, you may want to pause and make sure everyone feels comfortable with the main points of the lecture.*

# Small Group Interaction

*As Jonathan and Erica have become more aware of what Christians believe and why, they are starting to intentionally encourage open-ended spiritual conversations. As we enter back into their story, we will assume their familiarity with the main points of Andy's lecture.*

With Andy's message in mind, recall Trevor's intriguing remark to your question about what he is learning at school: "We are learning about the beginning of the universe in class. Not the fairy tale version with talking snakes."

1. There have been some seasons of tension between you and Trevor in the past. You and your spouse have been talking about how to build more trust with Trevor as he enters high school. Now that he's asking deeper questions about life you really want him to know it's safe for him to share his honest thoughts with you.

*Discuss together:*
- What approaches are most (or least) likely to strengthen trust with your son?

> *Depending on your group, the default responses to the narrative may vary widely. At this point, prioritize opening up the discussion rather than offering your personal evaluation of each person's approach.*

2. You say to Trevor, "I'm glad you brought this up, because it's an important topic. I think it's great that you've found this so interesting, even though I don't necessarily agree with everything you're learning. Tell me more about what your textbook says about where we came from."

Trevor responds, saying, "Mr. Hendricks says science has proven that we are here because of evolution. So if we know God didn't create everything, why keep telling the stories?"

*Discuss together:*
- How can you continue to affirm your interest in Trevor?
- What are some ways you could help Trevor see some of the logical implications of what he is saying?

> 👤 *Some people are naturally more interested in detailed conversations about science. Group members may be strongly committed to "young earth" or "old earth" perspectives and want to have a discussion about the right view of evolution. You may also have very strong views in this area. We encourage you to validate their interest in the subject while clarifying the distinctive focus of this study. Keep the group's attention on the attitude and approach that we bring to Trevor and the conversation. If you think it would be useful to discuss evolution or the age of the earth with your group, we would encourage you to table that topic until the end of the session, or schedule a separate time for that conversation.*

3. Your spouse jumps in and says, "Trevor, I think that's a great question. You know we didn't really stop to think about some of these things until we were much older, so I think it's wonderful that you're asking about them now. You may not remember, but both of us took a really long time before we were even ready to go to church. I guess neither of us got hung up on the question of evolution, but I will say that it's not as simple as what Mr. Hendricks says." Trevor looks intrigued. Your spouse continues, "I think the real issue here isn't our attitude towards science but whether or not God is there. Let me ask you something: do you think every person is equally valuable?"

Trevor quickly agrees: "Of course! Everyone knows that."

*Discuss together:*
- Sometimes Christians get labeled as "anti-science". How can we avoid this trap?
- What points from Andy's lecture could you bring into the conversation with your son?
- What questions would move the conversation forward in an open and respectful way?

---

4. You decide to share one idea you've learned from some recent reading. "Trevor, I recently read a quote from Richard Dawkins about this very issue. Do you know who he is?" Trevor says, "Yes, Mr. Hendricks mentions him a lot." You respond, "Well, he says that humans are just biological machines who do what their genes make us do. Life is nothing more than a ruthless competition to survive and get ahead. If that's all we are, how do you make sense of the idea that we're all equally valuable?"

Trevor is quiet. Finally, Alyssa breaks the silence. "Mom, can I have some dessert?" As the cake gets passed around, Trevor speaks up again. "You know, I hadn't really thought about that. But just because I don't know the answer doesn't mean we should believe whatever the Bible tells us."

*Discuss together:*
- What might Trevor *really* be saying? One of the skills we want to develop in our group is the ability to hear "the question underneath the question" so that we can engage in a more empathetic, respectful, and effective manner.

> *The focus should be trying to understand what Trevor is feeling here. Does he just not want to believe the Bible? Is he frustrated that he doesn't have a response? Does he resent his parents knowing more than he does on this?*

- Based on your group's perspective about where Trevor is coming from, what kinds of responses make the most sense? By contrast, what approaches might set you back?

> *One way you can push beyond the written story and challenge your group is to ask this question: "How will that answer work if Trevor takes it back to the classroom and shares it in front of his friends and Mr. Hendricks?"*

5. You feel a strong impression that you need to pray for your son. As you quietly ask God to give you guidance in navigating these unfamiliar waters and to open up Trevor's heart, you find yourself calmly saying, "Trevor, that's a great point. I'd love to talk about why we can trust the Bible too. I think we should stick to the other

question for now. We all agree that every human being is valuable. I think this is true because the Bible says we're all made in God's image. So what is it that makes human beings valuable if we are here as a result of random, unguided processes? I think this is one of the hardest questions to answer for someone who doesn't believe in God. Maybe Mr. Hendricks has an answer. But I'd love to talk about it more with you whenever you want."

Trevor lets out a little smile as he says, "Ok."

### Discuss together:
- What went well in this dinner conversation?
- If your group has time, consider doing a roleplay of your next conversation with Trevor. One person in the group can take Trevor's part and one (or two) members can stand in the place of Jonathan and Erica. Focus on practicing some of the approaches we've already identified as important (e.g., asking respectful questions, listening well).

> *We saw in our pilot groups that this exercise in many cases was the most helpful part of the lesson. We strongly encourage you to try this and if it goes well, incorporate it into upcoming lessons too.*

- In light of this conversation, how might you pray for your son?

> 👤 As you come to the end of the session, consider emphasizing again the two main points: 1. Because humans are made in God's image, we are all equally valuable. 2. With each person, we want to choose an approach that builds trust and opens up conversations.

## Your Notes:

## Closing Prayer

1. As you begin to get into the heart of this study, who is God reminding you to pray for? Share about the people in your life who you might start talking to about these deeper life issues.

> 👤 By sharing first, you may make it easier for other members of the group to share about the people they feel led to pray for.

2. How can your group pray for you? Discuss any personal prayer needs or concerns.

*After gathering all the prayer requests, take some time to pray for one another and those God has brought to mind.*

# Weekly Challenge:

> To develop any new habit, we typically need encouragement and social support. Continue to intentionally invite your group to join you in trying these exercises out. Feel free to modify them to best fit your context.

At this point, you have seen Andy discuss the link between human origins and human value. You've also practiced and discussed a conversation with Trevor on the same topic. Together, your group realized there were many good approaches available. In both of the examples we studied this week, the lecture and the conversation were built around two major questions:

- Where do you think humans come from?
- How does this perspective (whatever it is) justify human value?

There are natural, everyday moments to explore the deeper questions of life all around us. For instance, every day we encounter major news stories that inevitably become the topic of conversation with our family and friends. Whether it is in the local news, in politics, sports, entertainment, or global humanitarian crises, many of these stories assume that every human being is valuable. This week, we encourage you to pray for opportunities to ask open-ended questions and have meaningful conversations with your family, friends, and co-workers.

Next week those who are willing can share how God worked through their conversations.

# For Further Study

If you would like to do additional study on the biblical basis for this week's session, please see the "Next Steps" section at the end of your handbook.

## LEADER OVERVIEW FOR SESSION 3:

Before each session, we encourage you to read ahead, so that you are familiar with where each lecture and narrative is heading. Each session has many potential important points, but we encourage you to focus on just one or two main takeaways from each week's session.

This week, the lecture emphasizes one key idea: the image of God is the basis for human value, ethics, and dignity. The narrative emphasizes the emotional side of evangelism. Sometimes our emotional response to difficult personalities makes it harder to lovingly share our perspective.

The dialogue comes close to some potentially divisive topics. For instance, the contentious discussion around evolution and the purported "war" between science and faith. Instead of getting pulled into these familiar lines of exchange, keep bringing the conversation back to the primary questions of origin, meaning, morality, and destiny.

❗ **Your group should feel free to express how they might naturally respond to Uncle Bob's mean comments. Remaining open and safe for everyone to honestly share their current point of view is an invaluable part of the process.**

As you discuss this narrative, your group is learning not only what to say but how to say it. Your group should feel free to express how they might naturally respond to Uncle Bob's mean comments. Remaining open and safe for everyone to honestly share their current point of view is an invaluable part of the process. At the same time, we want to learn new habits of empathy, respect, and kindness in how we respond to people who are more provocative or difficult.

The importance of our example (and not just our words) can be raised by asking a simple question: What does Trevor notice? Does your group pick up on the contrast between your behavior towards Bob and his behavior towards you?

In some groups, this section could lead to a conversation about how previous mistakes are currently affecting the trust and quality of conversations with friends and family. Developing a long-term perspective on our friendships is a key value in the *Everyday Questions* experience.

If this week is the first session for anyone in your group, be sure to catch them up on the narrative. Give them a quick recap of who Jonathan and Erica are and what the group has discussed so far.

At the start of your time together, set aside some time to discuss how the weekly challenge went.

Finally, as you prepare for your meeting, remember to pray for your time together, and for each member of your group.

# Session 3: Origin

*Origin, Part 2:*
Andy Bannister

| | |
|---|---|
| Origin: | Where did everything come from? |
| Meaning: | Why are we here? |
| Morality: | What is right and wrong? |
| Destiny: | What happens when we die? |

**INTRODUCTION**

Uncle Bob had always been one of your favorite uncles. Growing up, the two of you were particularly close. Even though he is rough around the edges, he always had a soft spot for you. Because you knew he really disliked religion, it wasn't until last year that you were able to talk with him about your new faith. One weekend you worked up the courage to tell him about Jesus, and you pushed really hard on the importance of faith with him. Though he was polite at first, he eventually snapped at you to stop "shoving your religion down his throat." Though you have apologized for this on more than one occasion, you still feel that Uncle Bob is upset about how you've changed.

Ever since then, Uncle Bob has actively tried to discredit your faith. He particularly likes to spring tough questions on you in front of other people and see how you react.

You are at the family Christmas party when Bob starts talking about a documentary he just watched about evolution. He turns to you and says, "Looks like it's getting harder and harder to have faith in God in the face of all the evidence. Don't you think it makes so much more sense to agree with science and evolution?"

Every eye in the room is looking at you. You don't want to repeat the mistakes you've made in the past talking about faith with your Uncle Bob, but where do you start?

---

Andy's presentation will expand on the subject of origin. This week the focus is on how being made in God's image impacts our understanding of ethics and human dignity. As you listen to Andy's talk, consider how to apply his approach to your discussion with Uncle Bob.

*Before starting the video, have a member of your group open your time together in prayer.*

# Video Guide

This guide is intended to make it easy to take notes on Andy's message. The main ideas and quotes are outlined below for your convenience.

*Summary of Session Two:*
- The question of origins directly affects how we answer the question, "What does it mean to be human?"
- The atheistic explanation of origins generates significant problems.
- The biblical foundation of human origins is first found in Genesis 1:26-27, which establishes that humans are made in the image of God.
- Because we bear God's image, we can reasonably establish that all human beings are valuable.

*This week, we will discuss the relevance of God's image for ethics and human dignity.*

## Foundation for Ethics

*What is the basis for treating each other with compassion and dignity?*

### C.S. Lewis, "The Weight of Glory" [4]

There are no ordinary people. You have never talked to a mere mortal. Nations, cultures, arts, civilization—these are mortal, and their life is to ours as the life of a gnat. But it is immortals whom we joke with, work with, marry, snub, and exploit—immortal horrors or everlasting splendors.

...Next to the Blessed Sacrament itself, your neighbor is the holiest object presented to your senses.

---

[4] C.S. Lewis, *The Weight of Glory and Other Addresses* (New York: Macmillan, 1949).

# Foundation for Human Dignity

*Does human dignity actually exist?*

**The UN Declaration on Human Rights**
Recognition of the inherent dignity and of the equal and inalienable rights of all members of the human family is the foundation of freedom, justice and peace in the world.

*Where is human dignity located? How do we avoid being arbitrary in drawing the circle of dignity?*

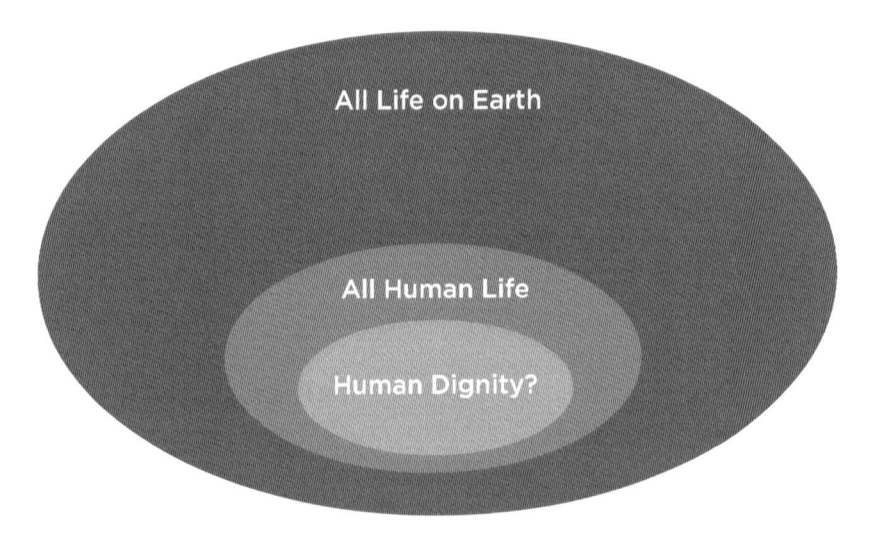

All Life on Earth

All Human Life

Human Dignity?

**Sam Harris, *The End of Faith*** [5]
The problem is that whatever attributes we use to differentiate between humans and animals; intelligence, language use, moral sentiments and so on, will equally differentiate between human beings themselves.

---

[5] Sam Harris, *The End of Faith: Religion, Terror, and the Future of Reason* (New York: W.W. Norton & Co., 2004).

**Rodney Stark, *The Triumph of Christianity*** [6]
> Amid this universal slavery, only one civilization ever rejected human bondage: Christendom. And it did it twice!

**Raimond Gaita, *A Common Humanity*** [7]
> We may say that all human beings are inestimably precious, that they are ends in themselves, that they are owed unconditional respect, that they possess inalienable rights, and, of course, that they possess inalienable dignity. In my judgment these are ways of trying to say what we feel a need to say when we are estranged from the conceptual resources we need to say it. Be that as it may: each of them is problematic and contentious. Not one of them has the simple power of the religious ways of speaking.

## Why Does the World Look the Way It Does?

## An Atheist Perspective

*One of the challenges for secular naturalism is to explain why human beings consistently go wrong in so many ways.*

**Randall Jarrell** [8]
> Most of us know, now, that Rousseau was wrong: that man, when you knock his chains off, sets up the death camps. Soon we shall know everything the 18th century didn't know, and nothing it did, and it will be hard to live with us.

---

[6] Rodney Stark, *The Triumph of Christianity: How the Jesus Movement Became the World's Largest Religion* (New York, N.Y: HarperOne, 2011).
[7] Raimond Gaita, *A Common Humanity: Thinking About Love and Truth and Justice* (London: Routledge, 2008), 23.
[8] Randall Jarrell, *New York Times Book Review* (August 23, 1953).

# A Christian Perspective

*Inherent in the word "image" is the idea of the word "reflection." We judge the quality of a mirror by how accurately it reflects our face. We are intended to reflect God's image.*

### C.S. Lewis, "The Weight of Glory"
> If we consider the unblushing promises of reward and the staggering nature of the rewards promised in the Gospels, it would seem that Our Lord finds our desires not too strong, but too weak. We are half-hearted creatures, fooling about with drink and sex and ambition when infinite joy is offered us, like an ignorant child who wants to go on making mud pies in a slum because he cannot imagine what is meant by the offer of a holiday at the sea. We are far too easily pleased.

*So what is the solution to our broken reflections?*

### Colossians 1:13-20

*We have a true, living, certain hope. We have a hope not for what God might do, but for what God has done: in Jesus, in the true image of God, in the cross.*

### Summary:

- The biblical truth that every person is made in the image of God provides a foundation for the ethical treatment of all people.
- The idea of universal human dignity is rooted in the biblical teaching that human beings are made the image of God.
- Atheistic worldviews struggle to explain why the world is broken and why people make bad decisions.

- The Christian understanding that we are broken reflections of God's image allows us to point people toward the ultimate hope of God's redemption.

> *Before going to the small group interaction, you may want to pause and make sure everyone feels comfortable with at least the main points of the lecture.*

# Small Group Interaction

As you gather your thoughts at the Christmas party, Andy's message about the image of God as the foundation for human value, ethics, and dignity rings in your ears. Uncle Bob pushes a little more, "Don't you get tired of having to convince yourself that what you believe is right when it constantly goes against the evidence? Are you really going to tell us we should take seriously the mythology of the Bible over the legitimacy of modern science?"

> *We have portrayed Uncle Bob in an intentionally provocative way. The main principle we hope that your group learns in this dialogue is how to respond in an emotionally healthy and loving way to someone who is hostile to their faith.*

1. As you look across the room, you see family members that you know come from a wide variety of spiritual backgrounds. Some are active Christians, others seem to jump from one trend to another, and many of them actively avoid discussing the topic. Then there's Uncle Bob.

*Discuss together:*
- What are some gracious ways to engage with Bob's challenge?
- What are some approaches that might close down the conversation?

---

2. As you think about how to respond, you're struck by the realization that the problem isn't finding what to say, but what not to say. You're starting to feel more confident as you realize how many good options there are to engage with Uncle Bob. But you want to make sure your response is directed at Bob and not just his argument. After pausing once more, you start out:

"Bob, you and I seem to understand the evidence very differently. I admit that I'm not an expert on the science behind the origin of the universe, and I don't know if either one of us is really prepared to get into the details of those debates. Regardless of your belief on where we all came from, other questions still need answers. For example, what makes us any different from other animals? We don't have a problem with lions taking down a giraffe on the savannah, right? But if a human did that to another human they'd be locked up. How do you justify that?"

Your Uncle Bob seems surprised by your question. He thinks for a minute, then says, "Well, it's evolution. Societies that survived and evolved were the ones where people didn't kill and eat each other. So now we all feel that it's wrong to kill another human being. Evolution is the reason we became empathetic; we don't need any fairy tales to tell us that it's wrong to hurt each other."

> *Depending on your group, you may have some members who do have expertise on the science behind the origin of the universe or the topic of evolution. However, remind your group that the focus is not a detailed scientific investigation. Instead, we are learning together how to build trust and open up conversations about God.*

*Discuss together:*
- How can you avoid getting sidetracked into a discussion about evolution?
- How does this first response to Uncle Bob tie into the points Andy raised in his lecture?

---

3. As much as you want to defend yourself from Bob's suggestion that you believe in fairy tales, you decide to take a positive approach. Speaking calmly, you say,

"I definitely agree that we shouldn't hurt each other. We all believe that every person deserves to be treated with respect and dignity. But it's hard to explain why that is if we only got here by evolution. You've quoted Sam Harris to me before. Even he has pointed out that it's really hard to define what makes humans unique. If it's by intelligence, then should we also say that people who are smarter are more valuable than others? That would mean newborn babies and disabled people have less value than the rest of us. It's actually only Christianity that can explain why every single human being is valuable. It's because every human being bears the image of God that they are worthy of our protection. I know we don't agree with each other on everything, but my faith in Christ is why I believe in the dignity of all people."

*Discuss together:*
- What are some other approaches you could take to respectfully raise the issues of ethics and human dignity?

---

4. Your Uncle Bob tries to turn the argument back on you. He becomes even more condescending. "You're seriously telling me that Christians are the only ones who care about protecting babies and

disabled people? See, this is what you Christians do. You think you're the only good people in the world and then you go around telling others how evil they are. If only you people took science seriously, there would be no more religion and we wouldn't have to deal with this kind of judgmental attitude."

*Discuss together:*
- When conversations become heated and personal, what are some of the potential issues at stake?

*To encourage open sharing, consider telling your group about a time when a conversation about faith became heated or personal for you, and what you learned from that experience.*

5. Realizing that the opportunity for a reasonable back-and-forth has passed, you decide to defuse the situation as best you can. You say, "Woah, Uncle Bob, that's not what I meant at all. I'm truly sorry if it came across that way. I think we agree that all people have unique value. What I'm saying is that only Christianity is able to explain why that is. That doesn't mean the only people who do good things are Christians. I know you do a lot of good things for our family and people in the community, and even though we disagree about God, we do agree about a lot of important moral values. Maybe we should pick this up another time? I'm always up for a good conversation with you."

Bob responds, "Yeah, yeah, ok, fine. We can talk about your made-up God whenever you want." As he walks away, you silently pray for him. As you do, you look over and see that Trevor has been listening carefully.

*Discuss together:*
What are some ways you might want to follow up this conversation...
- with your uncle Bob?
- with Trevor?
- with other family members?

*In next week's session, Stuart McAllister, a speaker with Ravi Zacharias International Ministries, will introduce us to some new insights on the topic of meaning.*

## Everyday Questions:

As a group, brainstorm some of the "everyday questions" you have heard or might hear on the topic of meaning. It's not terribly uncommon to hear questions that relate to meaning or purpose: Why did something bad happen? What do you want to do with your life? Are you happy? This subject is addressed all the time in popular culture. Discuss together some of the everyday questions that might naturally lead into a conversation on the topic of meaning.

## Your Notes:

# Closing Prayer

1. As Andy quoted from C.S. Lewis's essay "The Weight of Glory": There are no ordinary people. You have never talked to a mere mortal. Nations, cultures, arts, civilization—these are mortal, and their life is to ours as the life of a gnat. But it is immortals whom we joke with, work with, marry, snub, and exploit—immortal horrors or everlasting splendors.

Who are some of the people in your life who need to hear about Christ?

2. How can your group pray for you? Discuss any personal prayer needs or concerns.

*After gathering all the prayer requests, take some time to pray for one another and those God has brought to mind.*

# Weekly Challenge:

An important part of evangelism is the emotional experience of discussing (and disagreeing about) important topics. Ask God for opportunities to discuss the issues of human value and dignity. Find out from someone who isn't a Christian how they would explain why all human beings are of equal value. Make sure to approach these conversations with sincere curiosity, and not a goal to criticize their beliefs. Next week, we will have the opportunity to hear how God worked through your conversations.

# For Further Study

If you would like to do additional study on the biblical basis for this week's session, please see the "Next Steps" section at the end of your handbook.

Now to him who is able to do far more abundantly than all that we ask or think, according to the power at work within us, to him be glory in the church and in Christ Jesus throughout all generations, forever and ever. Amen.
—*Ephesians 3:20-21 (ESV)*

## LEADER OVERVIEW FOR SESSION 4:

Depending on the circumstances of your group, the narrative may hit quite close to home. You may already be praying for someone in the group, or one of their family members or close friends, who has received a terminal diagnosis. It may turn out that offering support for a group member who is going through a difficult season is more important than completing the planned lesson. Demonstrating a practical concern for one another is in many ways more important than talking about what, hypothetically, you would do in such a situation.

> **Demonstrating a practical concern for one another is in many ways more important than talking about what, hypothetically, you would do in such a situation.**

Some people in your group may sense that Jonathan doesn't do anything particularly noteworthy in leading Fred to a relationship with Christ. If this comes up in your discussion, celebrate! That's the point. The long-term, genuine friendship and trust that Jonathan has built with Fred is what gives him the credibility to share the gospel and invite his friend to know Christ. But ultimately, a spiritual transformation is God's work, and we are only one small part of the process.

The climax of this week's small group discussion involves sharing the gospel with your friend. If you are feeling unfamiliar with how you would personally do this, take some time to develop your understanding of what the gospel is and how you would share it in your own words. You can find good resources at RZIM.org and by asking your pastor for guidance. This preparation will serve you and your group well.

As in prior weeks, remember to discuss the weekly challenge together, and ask group members for any updates about the people and circumstances for which they've requested prayer.

This week's lesson is built around two important ideas:

- First, the central point of Stuart's lecture is that life is framed by stories. Meaning and hope naturally follow from understanding the Christian story.
- Second, the primary point of the narrative is that God is the author of salvation.

Practically, these two main points have many implications. For instance:

- There are no evangelism "tips and tricks" that can save someone; as Stuart says, "Christ did not come to make bad people good. He came to make dead people live."
- We are to be faithful and prepared to facilitate God's work in the lives of our family members, friends, and colleagues.
- When we understand that God is the author of salvation, we are more motivated to pray, together and on our own, for those we know and love.

# Session 4: Meaning

*Meaning, Part 1:*
Stuart McAllister

**INTRODUCTION**

| | |
|---|---|
| Origin: | Where did everything come from? |
| **Meaning:** | **Why are we here?** |
| Morality: | What is right and wrong? |
| Destiny: | What happens when we die? |

Every few weeks, you meet up with Fred, the company's attorney, to review various legal issues related to your business unit. He's a happy, successful guy who seems to get along with everyone. His office is dotted with pictures of his wife and three kids on vacations around the world and with celebrities he met while playing minor league baseball before law school. He's never been a religious person, but he's always worked hard and tried to do the right thing. You consider him to be one of your closest friends at the office.

This time, as the meeting progresses, you're surprised to notice that Fred is struggling to stay focused. As you put away your laptop at the end of the meeting, you pause and ask, "Fred, what's going on?" He looks like he is about to speak, but then stops. Tears fill his eyes and he looks down. After a minute he looks up. His voice is very shaky as he finally says, "The doctors say I've got stage four throat cancer." The words are coming slowly as he fights to keep his composure. "I don't know how long I have. And even if I make it, they say I might not be able to speak again. This is the hardest thing I've ever experienced and it's been really tough for my family too."

Fred's disclosure hits you in the gut. Why Fred? Why now? You know one of his daughters just got engaged and his son is about to graduate from high school. You sit with Fred in silence, overwhelmed with sadness, wondering what you could possibly say.

Fred seems to "have it all," but his diagnosis is waking him up to the need for a greater meaning in life. In this week's video, Stuart McAllister will share some powerful insights on the topic. At the conclusion of his message, we'll continue the conversation with Fred.

*Before starting the video, have a member of your group open your time together in prayer.*

> **Remember to pray for anyone known to your group who is in a similar situation as Fred.**

# Video Guide

This guide is intended to make it easy to take notes on Stuart's message. The main ideas and quotes are outlined below for your convenience.

### Summary of Session Three:

- The biblical truth that every person is made in the image of God provides a foundation for the ethical treatment of all people.
- The idea of universal human dignity is rooted in the biblical teaching that human beings are made in the image of God.
- Atheistic worldviews struggle to explain why the world is broken and why people make bad decisions.
- The Christian understanding that we are broken reflections of God's image allows us to point people toward the ultimate hope of God's redemption.

## The Christian View of Meaning

### John 1:1-5

#### Dr. Richard Dawkins [9]
DNA neither knows nor cares. DNA just is, and we dance to its music.

#### Romans 8:18-25

*Behind the very nature and power of the universe, there is a storied structure to life.*

#### John Piper, *Desiring God* [10]
The chief end of man is to glorify God by enjoying him forever.

## Other Views on Meaning

#### Charles Schulz, *Conversations* [11]
I don't know the meaning of life. I don't know why we are here...

## The Christian Narrative

### The Beginning

*There is a good Creator and a good creation.*

#### John 1:3

*We are in a great cosmic love story.*

---

[9] Richard Dawkins, *River Out of Eden: A Darwinian View of Life* (New York: Basic Books, 1995), 132.
[10] John Piper, *Desiring God: Meditations of a Christian Hedonist* (Colorado Springs, CO : Multnomah Books, 2011).
[11] Charles M. Shulz, *Conversations*, ed. M Thomas Inge (Jackson: University Press of Mississippi, 2000), 116.

# The Fallen World

### Romans 8:20-22

### Mark Twain, *Tom Sawyer, Detective* [12]
... oh, you don't quite know what it is you do want, but it just fairly makes your heart ache, you want it so!

### George MacDonald [13]
Man finds it hard to get what he wants, because he does not want the best; God finds it hard to give, because he would give the best, and man will not take it.

# The Human Condition

### Romans 3:23
...for all have sinned and fall short of the glory of God.

### Ecclesiastes 1:1-2, 3:11

*We have infinite longings but finite capacities. The human condition without God is one of restlessness and torment.*

# The Good News

*There is a Creator, there is a broken universe, and there is a Redeemer.*

### Titus 3:4-7

---

[12] Mark Twain, *Tom Sawyer, Detective* (Lanham, MD: Start Publishing LLC, 2015).
[13] George MacDonald, *Unspoken Sermons* (New York: Cosimo Classics, 2007), 207.

**C.S. Lewis, *Mere Christianity*** [14]
If I find in myself a desire which no experience in this world can satisfy, the most probable explanation is that I was made for another world.

## The Happy Ending

### Revelation 21:1-5

*Hope is part of having a meaningful life.*

**Lewis Smedes, *Keeping Hope Alive*** [15]
Keep hoping, you keep living. Stop hoping, you die. Inside.

*The resurrection brings up the greatest suffering of life and invests it with meaning and transcends death by giving us eternal hope. Death does not have the last word. In the end of this story, God is supreme.*

**Summary:**

- Answers to questions of meaning must be both objectively real (describing reality as it truly is) and existentially satisfying (applicable to the lives we live).
- The Christian view of meaning places us within God's cosmic love story.
- Other narratives that focus on "finding our meaning within ourselves" don't provide a strong foundation for a meaningful life.

---

[14] CS Lewis, *Mere Christianity* (New York: HarperOne, 2012).
[15] Lewis Smedes, *Keeping Hope Alive: For a Tomorrow We Cannot Control* (Nashville: Thomas Nelson, Inc., 1998).

- The Christian narrative begins with God's perfect creation, recognizes the fallen world, diagnoses the human condition, delivers the good news of the gospel, and brings hope in God's redemptive ending for all creation.

> *Before going to the small group interaction, you may want to pause and make sure everyone feels comfortable with at least the main points of the lecture.*

## Small Group Interaction

You and Fred sit in silence for a few moments. You're fighting back tears of your own as you try to think of what to say. Finally, Fred looks up at you and says, "I'm sorry I didn't tell you sooner, but I'm so used to handling these things on my own."

1. As you think about the stakes for Fred, you know this is a critical conversation. Fred trusts you. How will you love your friend in this difficult circumstance?

*Discuss together:*
- How would you respond to a friend in this situation?
- What are some of the hard times you have been (or are going) through?
- In what ways have you experienced God's purposes even in the midst of suffering?

> 👤 *Encourage your group to be real and authentic in processing this conversation. A primary learning objective is that evangelism is a means of expressing our love for God and others, and therefore, it cannot be something we do in a way that is inconsiderate, hasty, formulaic, or otherwise insensitive to our friends.*

2. For the next twenty minutes, you ask more questions and actively listen to him share about how the diagnosis is affecting both him and his family. But then Fred says, "You know, I've hardly slept since I found out. I've never really worried about the deeper meaning behind things, but now what keeps me up at night is wanting to know why."

You pause and gently ask, "Before all of this happened, what would you have said is the purpose of your life?"

*Discuss together:*
- How would you explain the Christian perspective on meaning and purpose?
- In particular, how does the Christian story help us make sense of difficult experiences?

---
---
---
---
---

3. Fred looks down at the carpet. He says, "Until I got the news, I figured I had everything a man could want. But still." Waving his hands at all the pictures and awards around his office, he continues, "You see all this, but the truth is, there have been times when I've wondered how I can have everything and still not feel satisfied."

Fred's comment resonates with you because you had some similar thoughts just a few years before. You open up, saying, "Do you remember me telling you I had become a Christian?" Fred nods. "I was happy for you, but didn't really get it." You smile remembering the conversation when you told him. "Before that happened, I was actually asking some of these same questions. It started when I got my promotion. I always thought that working hard and being successful would make me happy. But a few weeks into the new position, I realized I was still missing something. At the same time, Erica seemed to be more content than ever before, and so I decided to try going to church with her. That's where I realized: there are a lot of good things in life, but none of them can completely fulfill us."

### Discuss together:
- Stuart McAllister mentioned that, "We have infinite longings but finite capacities." What are the common ways that we – and our friends and family – try to find meaning and hope apart from God?

---
---
---
---

*Some other themes that may surface or that you may want to suggest: favorite sports teams, being 'the best' at something, the success or behavior of your children, politics, and/or financial security.*

4. What you're saying clearly hits home for Fred. "That's exactly what it is. It's the sense that I'm not fulfilled. So you're saying you found it at church. What does that mean?"

*Discuss together:*
- When someone asks you to explain either why you go to church or why you are a Christian, what do you say?

_____
_____
_____
_____
_____
_____
_____

5. Pausing to take stock of what Fred is asking, you quietly pray for God to guide your heart and your words. "I think the thing that helped me understand it best was a book by C.S. Lewis. He said that if I have desires for something that can't be met in this world, it makes sense to think I was made for another world. I kept thinking about it, and I realized that ultimately, none of my dreams meant anything without God. But if God had a reason for making us, then my life has a purpose — and hope.

"And then, each week at church, they were always praying and saying that God hears us. So I thought I would try it out. I started to pray and just asked God to help me. And that's when it all came together. I realized God loved me, and that I was made to love him too."

Fred looks reflective. He says, "This is really new for me. But how does it come together? I find it hard to believe that God could love me."

You say, "Anyone can know God's love. The Bible says, 'For God so loved the world that he gave his one and only Son' — that's Jesus — 'that whoever believes in him might not perish but have eternal life.' So Fred, this is available to you as well."

Fred is hanging onto every word, "I need that. There's something inside me telling me that this is exactly what I need. What do I do?"

*Discuss together:*
- How would you explain the gospel to a friend?
- If someone asked you to help them become a Christian, what would you say? What would you do?

---
---
---

> *These questions are some of the most important questions of the material so far. If members of your group aren't comfortable with their understanding of the gospel or how they would share it with their friends, they are unlikely to be confident evangelists. Take your time with these questions and gently encourage everyone to have a clear understanding of what it would look like for them to share the good news. Be prepared with some additional resources from either your pastor or RZIM to explain the gospel.*

6. It seems clear that the Holy Spirit is speaking to Fred. You haven't said much about what it means to follow Christ so you try to explain it as clearly as you can. "You need to talk to God and tell him. He's made you and he wants a relationship with you. What you've told me is that you've always pretty much ignored God, but I believe he has been pursuing you. The fulfillment you're looking for doesn't come from religion, but from God giving us new life. That's what you were made for and that's where you will be satisfied.

"The verse I quoted to you said that God gave his Son so that we could have eternal life. The reason is that God is perfect and so we have to be made perfect to know him. Jesus accomplished this for us. He lived a perfect life, died on the cross for all we've done wrong, and rose again from the dead. God has promised that if we call out to him, asking Jesus to forgive us and lead us, that he will save us and give us hope.

"So you just talk to God. Tell him, 'Jesus, please forgive me for everything I've done wrong and for always ignoring you. I believe that you created me and died for me and I want to live for you. I want to know you and I want to serve you. Please show me how to be the man you made me to be.'"

Fred is wiping tears from his eyes. He's not even trying to look professional. He chokes out, "Ok, give me a minute. I've never really prayed before, but I feel so strongly that this is true. I know I need God." As you see him bow his head, you start to pray.

### Discuss together:
- If one of your friends became a Christian, what would you do next?

---

*If at all possible, discuss how you (or other group members) have come alongside new believers as they have grown in their understanding of what it means to follow Jesus.*

## Your Notes:

## Closing Prayer

1. Share any updates about your family and friends that your group is praying for.

2. Share any updates on your own life that you would like the group to pray about.

## Weekly Challenge:

This week, you may spend time with people just like Fred in this story. Ask God to give you the spiritual awareness and opportunity to listen, to ask questions, and to see friends come into a personal knowledge of God.

In these conversations, there may be opportunities to ask the deeper questions of life. For instance:
- Do you think God has a purpose for your life?
- Do you think this is all there is?
- What would you say is the point of it all?

Next week, we will have the opportunity to hear how God worked through your conversations.

## For Further Study

If you would like to do additional study on the biblical basis for this week's session, please see the "Next Steps" section at the end of your handbook.

## LEADER OVERVIEW FOR SESSION 5:

This narrative highlights two approaches to evangelism. The initial exchange with Sandra is handled with wisdom and respect. At the same time, Jill's attempt to persuade Sandra seems to backfire. Comparing and contrasting yours and Jill's approaches can lead your group to a new level of awareness about how even our well-intentioned efforts can nevertheless be ineffective.

As your group learns about Sandra, many people in your group may recognize her character in someone they know. She is expressing what may be called a "shopping cart" approach to developing a worldview. Her cart is filled with a sampling of what looks good to her from many different religions and worldviews. Part of what your group may realize in this session is that there are hundreds of different approaches to spirituality. That means that in today's world, evangelism is not a simple matter of learning what to say to "a new age person" because there may be great variety from one person's beliefs to the next, even if they're using the same terms. We aim to respond to Sandra based on what she personally believes, not on the basis of what category she fits into.

> **Comparing and contrasting approaches can lead your group to a new level of awareness about how even our well-intentioned efforts can nevertheless be ineffective.**

The other challenge your group may face with Sandra is making sense of what she means. Some familiar terms she uses seem to have been given slightly different meanings. Encourage your group to think about questions they could ask Sandra to better understand her point of view, to better grasp where Sandra might be coming from, and to share about the potential frustration of interacting with someone whose communication style makes it difficult to understand what they actually believe.

As in previous weeks, before discussing this week's content, we encourage you to review the weekly challenge from last week's session.

[33] And when the demon had been cast out, the mute man spoke. And the crowds marveled, saying, "Never was anything like this seen in Israel." [34] But the Pharisees said, "He casts out demons by the prince of demons." [35] And Jesus went throughout all the cities and villages, teaching in their synagogues and proclaiming the gospel of the kingdom and healing every disease and every affliction. [36] When he saw the crowds, he had compassion for them, because they were harassed and helpless, like sheep without a shepherd. [37] Then he said to his disciples, "The harvest is plentiful, but the laborers are few; [38] therefore pray earnestly to the Lord of the harvest to send out laborers into his harvest."

—Matthew 9:33-38

# Session 5: Meaning

*Meaning, Part 2:*
Stuart McAllister

**INTRODUCTION**

> Origin: Where did everything come from?
> **Meaning: Why are we here?**
> Morality: What is right and wrong?
> Destiny: What happens when we die?

Once Trevor and Alyssa were both in school, you decided to begin pursuing a degree by taking some night classes. All you've been able to manage is one class per semester. This term you are enrolled in Introduction to Philosophy. Every Tuesday night, you've been on campus listening to Dr. Sullivan's lectures and engaging in the class discussions. This week's topic is the meaning of life.

Class always begins with a student-led discussion. This week your group leader is Sandra, whose enthusiasm and personality seem to draw everyone towards her. As your group gathers together, you happen to overhear her sharing with a friend that the divorce papers finally came through last week.

In the discussion group, Sandra leads off by saying, "I believe we are all made to fulfill our purpose. Each of us has a spark of god inside, and we must find it and allow our light to shine on others. I help people find their purpose through meditation and relaxation at the place I work."

As the group shares, Sandra listens attentively and offers an affirming response to everyone as they describe their meaning of life. As the last person to share, you start to say, "Well, I am a Christian." But before you can go any further, Sandra cuts you off, "You know, Jesus is one of my biggest inspirations. Well, isn't it amazing how we all basically believe the same thing! My heart tells me we're all really going to get along!"

You feel frustrated by how Sandra has misunderstood you. At the same time, now it's hard to know how to disagree without sounding disagreeable. What should you do?

*Before starting the video, have a member of your group open your time together in prayer.*

> **Ask if anyone in the group knows someone like Sandra. The more you can connect these hypothetical scenarios to actual conversations and people, the better.**

## Video Guide

This guide is intended to make it easy to take notes on Stuart's message. The main ideas and quotes are outlined below for your convenience.

### *Summary of Session Four:*

- Answers to questions of meaning must be both objectively real (describing reality as it truly is) and existentially satisfying (applicable to the lives we live.)
- The Christian view of meaning places us within God's cosmic love story.
- Other narratives that focus on "finding our meaning within ourselves" don't provide a strong foundation for a meaningful life.
- The Christian narrative begins with God's perfect creation, recognizes the fallen world, diagnoses the human condition, delivers the good news of the Gospel, and brings hope in God's redemptive ending for all creation.

Colossians 4:5-6

# Asking Questions

*Christians don't deny that life is complex. Our witness is tested by whether or not, in the biggest sense of things, Christianity explains life.*

## Questions About Reality and Truth

*What do I mean when I say the word "truth"?*

### Os Guinness, *Time for Truth* [16]
In the biblical view, truth is that which is ultimately, finally, and absolutely real...

## Questions About Purpose and Vanity of Life

*If there is no meaning in life, there is no "how" to live life either.*

### Ecclesiastes 1:12-14

### *The Dhammapada* [17]
The things of this semiotic world are all illusion, like a dream. For everyone looks, but where is the substance?

### Algernon Swinburne, "The Hymn of Man" [18]
Glory to Man in the highest! for Man is the master of things.

---

[16] Os Guinness, *Time for Truth: Living Free In a World of Lies, Hype and Spin* (Grand Rapids, MI: Baker Publishing Group, 2002), 78.
[17] Translated by Edward Conze (Penguin Classics 1959).
[18] Algernon Swinburne, "The Hymn of Man" in *Swinburne's Poems* (New York: Thomas Y. Crowell & Co., 1906).

*It is important to clarify what we're talking about. We look for the "cries of the heart."*

### T.S. Eliot, "Burnt Norton" [19]
Go, go go, said the bird: human kind
Cannot bear very much reality.

## Questions About Mortality

### Winston Churchill [20]
Any man who says he's not afraid of death is a liar.

*What happens when things go wrong?*

## The Importance of Good Questions

*We ask questions not to be smart, but to listen for how people respond.*

### Matthew 19:16-22

*We ask questions to see what's under the surface:*

### Václav Havel [21]
The tragedy of modern man is not that he knows less and less about the meaning of his own life, but that it bothers him less and less.

*People will do anything to avoid questions. We have to get the questions into their conscience because that will start the journey.*

---

[19] T.S. Eliot, "Burnt Norton" in *Four Quartets* (Orlando, FL: Harcourt, Inc., 1943).
[20] Quoted in Os Guinness, *The Journey: Our Quest For Faith and Meaning* (Colorado Springs, CO: NavPress, 2001).
[21] Quoted in Os Guinness, *The Journey: Our Quest For Faith and Meaning* (Colorado Springs, CO: NavPress, 2001).

**Woody Allen, *Manhattan***
People in Manhattan are constantly creating these unnecessary neurotic problems for themselves...

*We need to listen and respond; not react.*

**1 Peter 3:15**

*If Christianity doesn't answer the questions truthfully, accurately, and really, why would we believe it?*

**Thomas Morris, *Making Sense of It All*** [22]
All the genuine unhappiness in this world is a sign that true happiness is not found within its confines...

## Contrasts and Alternatives

*As communicators we must learn to illustrate with things that people can see and relate to. We can use other voices to say the same things.*

**Ernest Becker, *The Denial of Death*** [23]
Thus the plight of modern man: a sinner with no word for it ...

**Bertrand Russell** [24]
I wrote with passion and force because I really thought I had a gospel...

**Albert Camus** [25]
Atheism is a cruel long-term business. I believe I have gone through it to the end.

---

[22] Thomas V. Morris, *Making Sense of It All: Pascal and The Meaning of Life* (Grand Rapids, MI: Wm. B. Eerdmans Publishing Co., 1992), 134.
[23] Ernest Becker, *The Denial of Death* (New York: Free Press Paperbacks, 1973), 198.
[24] Quoted in Os Guinness, *The Journey: Our Quest For Faith and Meaning* (Colorado Springs, CO: NavPress, 2001).
[25] While credited to Camus in this lecture, quote is originally from Jean-Paul Sartre, *Les Mots* (Paris: Gallimard, 1964).

*Your job is to witness, not to convert anybody. The Spirit convicts. God must open eyes and hearts. Our hope is for clarity and comprehension that through what we say, the gospel will point them towards the King.*

**Summary:**
- Self-made narratives often don't prove satisfying in real-life situations, but the Christian narrative provides a framework to explain all of life.
- Not all ideas are of equal value and not all can be received. We must learn to ask good questions and to listen carefully to tell the difference.
- Belief does not make something true; only correspondence to reality does.
- If there is no meaning in life, there is no "how" to live life either.
- We have to challenge ways of seeing the world without being argumentative. We ask questions not to be smart, but to listen for how people respond.

*Before going to the small group interaction, you may want to pause and make sure everyone feels comfortable with at least the main points of the lecture.*

# Small Group Interaction

Before you can respond, Sandra claps her hands, looks at everyone with a big smile, and introduces the next question for the evening's discussion. "Ok, so basically we all agree that we need to find our own path to happiness. But how do you find that for yourself?" Then, without a pause, Sandra immediately answers her own question, "I think this one is pretty easy! So many of us are distracted and worried about everything going on. But, you know, it is so relaxing and peaceful to take some 'me time' and meditate. When we listen to our hearts, we will find our own divine, wonderful purpose for being happy. What does everyone think about that?"

***Discuss together:***
- What are some questions you could ask Sandra to open up the conversation?
- Have you ever felt annoyed or aggravated by someone when spiritual topics come up? What are some practical ways to handle these frustrating experiences?

_____

_____

_____

_____

_____

_____

2. As a few people in the group thoughtfully nod their heads in appreciation for Sandra's comforting words, you decide to jump in with a question. "Sandra, that is a really interesting approach. One thing I noticed in the articles that we read this week was that the authors came from so many perspectives. The one from the Muslim imam said that our purpose comes from submitting to Allah. The French philosopher said that our sense of purpose is just an illusion that promotes survival of the species. What do you say to people who disagree with your definition of meaning?"

Sandra responds quickly. She says, "I think we use different terms but we mean the same thing. The Muslim follows Allah, you follow Jesus, I follow the divine spark. Isn't it all basically the same? You should know this is what Jesus taught. Love our neighbors and be happy."

*Discuss together:*
- How have you experienced "Jesus" being incorporated into other belief systems?
- Based on your understanding of Sandra's perspective, how would you respond to her?

---

3. As you pause to pray for Sandra, you say, "I agree that following Jesus will ultimately make us happy. But I think that what's most important is that we do what God wants us to do. Jesus wants us to fulfill our purpose in life, but he also defines that for us. If the purpose of life was just to be happy, Jesus never would have died on the cross for our sins. As a Christian, I think God's primary purpose for me is to love God and love others, even when it is hard or inconvenient."

*Discuss together:*
- Have you ever experienced someone misquoting Jesus's words?
- What questions could you ask Sandra to better understand her perspective?

---

4. Sandra seems unfazed. "Well sure, but I think we're just defining happiness differently. Jesus was happy to die on the cross because he was helping people. That's what made him happy. Happy doesn't have to mean easy and comfortable. We all have to do things that are difficult, but those things should make us feel good. Even if it hurts, we're still fulfilling our own unique purpose."

*Discuss together:*
- What can you do when the very meaning of words seems to be in question?
- In what ways does our culture link the ideas of "being happy" and "fulfilling our purpose" in life?

---

5. You realize that Sandra's view of Christianity is something she has thought about quite a bit. You decide to take a moment to ask God for wisdom and carefully choose your next words.

While you consider what you might say, another student, Jill, speaks up. "Sandra, I like the idea that we should all keep our own purpose in mind as we think about how we live our lives and how to make ourselves and others happy. But where I get stuck is when my happiness comes in conflict with someone else's. What about things like abortion? If it's really a question of happiness, can't we say that the happiness of the mother and the happiness of the baby are in conflict?"

*Discuss together:*
- What cautions should we keep in mind before bringing up controversial topics like abortion?

---

*This question is designed to remind people that when talking with someone you don't know, it's extremely important to be careful when using examples that may be controversial. Your aim is to point people towards Christ, and this could put a new barrier in place that wasn't there before.*

- In this case, do you think it was a good idea to use this example? What other examples could you have used to illustrate the competing happiness of individuals?

> *Some members of your group (or you!) may feel that Jill's example is a good idea. If this is the case, consider an open-ended approach to discussing the pros and the cons of using controversial examples. At the same time, be mindful that there may be members of your group who have had an abortion or encouraged a partner to have one. This is a conversation where grace and sensitivity are particularly important.*

6. Sandra winces when Jill says the word abortion, but quickly recovers. You don't think Jill noticed, but you sense that this is a very sensitive topic for Sandra. Her uncharacteristically sharp response seems to confirm your initial perception: "Abortion is a choice for the mother. A fetus is not a person. But we really can't get into that tonight. Let's stick to the assigned discussion questions."

As she moves on to the next question, her smile returns. But it's not quite as bright as it was earlier.

*Discuss together:*
- What can you do when you realize that a discussion has unintentionally caused pain for someone?
- What next steps might you take to continue the conversation with Sandra?

*In next week's session, Michael Ramsden, a speaker with Ravi Zacharias International Ministries, will introduce us to some new insights on the topic of morality*

## Everyday Questions:

As a group, brainstorm some of the "everyday questions" you have heard or might hear on the topic of morality. It's not terribly uncommon to hear questions that relate to right or wrong: They probably more often sound like statements than questions. Controversial issues that frequently become heated often center around morality. We frequently hear discussion of injustice or violations of rights, or passioned pleas for something to change in our society or our politics. Discuss together some of the everyday questions that might naturally lead into a conversation on the topic of morality.

## Your Notes:

## Closing Prayer

Stuart concluded his lecture with these words:

> As we go out there to talk about meaning, we tell biblical stories, we tell stories of others, we tell our own story. We remember that your job is to witness, not to convert anybody. The Spirit convicts. God must open eyes and hearts. Our hope is for clarity and comprehension that through what we say, the gospel will point them towards the King. To clear away the clutter and give them an answer, an answer that's rationally coherent, an answer that has evidential backing behind it and that is experientially relevant because that's what the gospel does.

We pray together to realize our dependence on God, to ask for his strength to be faithful, and to invite him to do the work of changing lives.

1. Share any updates about your family and friends that your group is praying for.

2. Share any updates on your own life that you would like the group to pray about.

## Weekly Challenge:

As a group, make plans to reach out together and welcome people who are not yet part of a church community. There's no objective except to gather people and build friendships with new people or deepen existing relationships. Of course, we should pray that God naturally creates opportunities for discussion about things we've been learning in this study.

> *This is a great opportunity to share ownership and leadership of the group with others. For those group members who love showing hospitality, encourage them to take the lead on organizing this social event. For instance, you might organize an informal barbeque at someone's home, or a picnic at a local park, or participate together in a service project in your community.*
>
> *We certainly hope good conversations will arise at the event with friends who aren't part of your church, but it's very important that it doesn't feel forced, or that the invitees don't feel like they were "tricked" into coming to an event just so your group members could evangelize.*

## For Further Study

If you would like to do additional study on the biblical basis for this week's session, please see the "Next Steps" section at the end of your handbook.

## LEADER OVERVIEW FOR SESSION 6:

This week's conversation emphasizes the importance of trust and long-term friendships. One of the reasons for highlighting evangelism in these contexts is that while it's easy to see why genuineness and authenticity matter with really close friends, it's also important to approach others with the same degree of respect and sincerity. By adopting this same approach to all of our conversations about faith, we are more likely to win people's trust and be enabled to have open-ended discussions about the universal questions of origin, meaning, morality, and destiny.

❗ **As you prepare for this week's session, think about the people God has placed in your life where you need to renew hope that they might become more interested in spiritual issues.**

Sometimes these friendships can seem "off-limits" to evangelism, and as this narrative reveals, there are seasons where discussing God or church could be inappropriate. At the same time, we want to remain prayerful and prepared to take measured risks to open up the discussion with our friends when it makes sense to do so. As you prepare for this week's session, think about the people God has placed in your life where you need to renew hope that they might become more interested in spiritual issues.

This lesson also deals with the somewhat sensitive issue of people having been hurt by the church or by individual Christians. There are two responses from your group that we want to avoid. The first is to feel defensive and offer excuses for whatever might have happened in the past. The focus of the conversation should not be on whether or not Gina's response is merited. The second response is to take the opposite perspective and become overly critical of the church or Christians. Again, the focus should be on how we respectfully and lovingly engage with people who feel they have been hurt by individual Christians or the church generally at some point in the past.

> **The focus should be on how we respectfully and lovingly engage with people who feel they have been hurt by individual Christians or the church generally at some point in the past.**

Before discussing this week's content, if your group has not yet hosted a social event for your friends, continue to keep this discussion alive. Alternatively, if you did do something as a group to engage with people who don't yet know God, be sure to celebrate the effort and discuss how it went with one another.

Continue to pray for your group members and for your meeting.

# Session 6: Morality

*Morality, Part 1:*
Michael Ramsden

## INTRODUCTION

| | |
|---|---|
| Origin: | Where did everything come from? |
| Meaning: | Why are we here? |
| **Morality:** | **What is right and wrong?** |
| Destiny: | What happens when we die? |

At the end of a long week, you and your spouse are out on a double date with your next door neighbors, Tom and Gina. After you moved into the neighborhood, they became two of your most loyal friends. Trevor stayed with them when Alyssa was born. Gina and the kids practically lived with you when Tom's mother was sick and he was gone every weekend to take care of her.

When you began going to church, they seemed uncomfortable. Gina was especially vocal in her concerns, so in the last five years, there have only been a few occasions to discuss faith. Each time it has created tension. All you really know is that her strong feelings about Christianity come from some difficult experiences in her childhood. Because of this, you have quietly but consistently prayed for Tom and Gina, trusting that God will eventually create opportunities.

During dinner, Gina brings up a topic that makes you wonder whether God might be providing an occasion to broach the subject. She and Tom have always taught their kids how to make good choices, but tonight she shares how it has become increasingly hard to explain to her daughter why some of her decisions are wrong.

You watch her closely as you begin, "Gina, I know we sort of have a mutual understanding not to talk about God, but in this case… well, that is where we base our understanding of right and wrong."

Gina starts to shake her head. "Look, you both aren't like this, but I just have a very low opinion of how Christians live out their 'morality.' There are some really bad Christians, and then they are super judgmental about how I'm supposed to live my life. I'm sorry but I just don't see it."

*Before starting the video, have a member of your group open your time together in prayer.*

> **Remember that there may be members in your own group who have had painful experiences in the past, possibly related to Christianity or the church. Be sensitive to this as your group discusses this week's content.**

# Video Guide

This guide is intended to make it easy to take notes on Michael's message. The main ideas and quotes are outlined below for your convenience.

### Summary of Session Five:
- Self-made narratives often don't prove satisfying in real-life situations, but the Christian narrative provides a framework to explain all of life.
- Not all ideas are of equal value and not all can be received. We must learn to ask good questions and to listen carefully to tell the difference.
- Belief does not make something true; only correspondence to reality does.
- If there is no meaning in life, there is no "how" to live life either.
- We have to challenge ways of seeing the world without being argumentative. We ask questions not to be smart, but to listen for how people respond.

## Love and Judgment

*Is God morally trustworthy or not?*

*What kind of God do we worship? Does God change from one day to another?*

Are there two Gods in the Bible?
- The God of the Old Testament who is a God of war, wrath, and vengeance.
- The God of the New Testament who is a God of love, mercy, and kindness.

*In reality, the exact same words are used to talk of God's love and justice in the Old Testament as in the New Testament.*

## The Book of Jonah

*Jonah goes to Nineveh and preaches, and everyone repents. Jonah sees a massive-scale revival in a major metropolis, but what is his reaction?*

**Jonah 4:1-3**
But to Jonah this seemed very wrong, and he became angry. He prayed to the LORD, "Isn't this what I said, LORD, when I was still at home? That is what I tried to forestall by fleeing to Tarshish. I knew that you are a gracious and compassionate God, slow to anger and abounding in love, a God who relents from sending calamity. Now, Lord, take away my life, for it is better for me to die than to live."

Jonah's complaint: God is too forgiving, too kind, too loving.

## Judgment and Revenge

*We often confuse judgment with revenge.*

The James Bond villain

*We want to see the villain come to a painful end, not only to justice. We must not get justice and revenge confused; they are not the same.*

*Why does God judge in the first place? Is it unreasonable?*

## The Nature of Love

*What do we mean by love?*

### *Pride and Prejudice*

*Darcy claims to love Elizabeth even though it goes against his will, his reason, and his own better character. She dismisses this declaration because he claims to love her against all better judgment.*

*True love doesn't exist in the absence of judgment; true love exists in the presence of it.*

*We go around projecting an image of ourselves to other people, but then people fall in love with that image of us rather than the reality.*

*The words "I love you" are meaningful when the person who speaks them knows the real you.*

*God sees us as we really are. He doesn't have an image of you. He knows you.*

*The message of the gospel is not that God came into this world to rescue good people.*

**1 John 4:10**
This is love: not that we loved God, but that he loved us and sent his Son as an atoning sacrifice for our sins.

**Romans 5:8**
But God demonstrates his own love for us in this: While we were still sinners, Christ died for us.

*God loved us knowing exactly what we were like, and his love makes us lovely.*

*Do you know that kind of love in your life?*

*Love and judgment are not categories that exclude each other; they inform each other.*

*Is it possible that love is dying in this world because we don't live in sufficiently close community to know what people are really like?*

**Summary:**
- God's love and God's judgment are the same in the Old Testament and the New Testament.
- We often confuse justice with vengeance, but they are not the same.
- Love does not exist in the absence of judgment; it exists in the presence of it.
- God knows exactly what we're like and still loves us.
- Love and judgment do not exclude each other; they inform each other.

> *Before going to the small group interaction, you may want to pause and make sure everyone feels comfortable with at least the main points of the lecture.*

## Small Group Interaction

Gina's comment about "super judgmental Christians" stings a little, but you're thankful she doesn't see you that way. Though it is still clearly a sensitive topic for her, it seems like this is the most open she and Tom have been to discussing God with you.

1. While her perspective is hard to hear, you want Gina and Tom to be honest and open with you about religion and their view of God.

*Discuss together:*
- How might the close ties between you and your neighbors affect the kind of conversation you can have over dinner?
- What might be at stake for Tom or Gina if they decide to start following Jesus?

_____
_____
_____
_____

> *Encourage your group to think through the many ways that becoming a Christian changes your life: your reputation, your purpose in life, your worldview, your spirituality, your weekend habits, your finances, etc.*

2. Your spouse responds first. "I understand why you would say that. I have a cousin who is always posting things on social media about how awful Christians are. And I used to think the same thing, though maybe not as passionately as he does. And sadly there are people in the church who fit the negative stereotype. But it's also ironic to see how hateful my cousin's language can be when he's criticizing Christians for being hateful. Don't you think we all end up passing judgment in one way or another?"

Gina hesitates, then says, "Ok, fair enough. But like you said, the perception that Christians are pretty judgmental is out there for a reason. Why do Christians feel like they have to tell others how to live?"

*Discuss together:*
- In what ways do you personally experience or see evidence of the stereotype that Christians are judgmental?

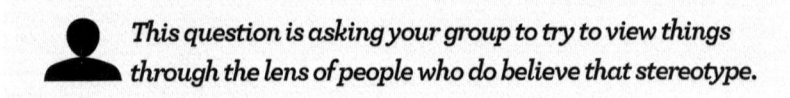

*This question is asking your group to try to view things through the lens of people who do believe that stereotype.*

- How have these perceptions hindered your own desire or opportunity to share your faith with others?

*Try to avoid the conversation spiraling down into, ironically, a judgmental conversation about how judgmental other Christians are.*

3. You decide that instead of answering Gina with an explanation, it might be more helpful to ask her a question instead. You say, "That's a great question. But I think before answering that question we should ask if it's ever okay to tell someone else they should change how they live?  In other words, is it also judgmental to tell other people not to be judgmental?"

*Discuss together:*
- What other questions could you ask Gina?
- What could be some risks of jumping straight into giving an answer?

4. As Gina thinks about what you've said, her husband Tom speaks up. "Well, I think the answer is pretty obvious. If you're in favor of tolerance, you have to be against being judgmental. We want to create a better society and that means we need to find a way to get along with one another. It's pretty simple: if you're for tolerance, you're against intolerance."

*Discuss together:*
- Who or what informs your view about what "a better society" would look like?
- How can tolerance help—or hinder—our ability to get along with one another?

> 👤 *The goal of these questions is to get your group thinking about what is at stake for Tom and Gina, and how your own Christian convictions intersect with their point of view. If the conversation turns to extended political points of view, for instance, you may need to steer the conversation back to the flow of the narrative.*

5. Your spouse jumps in to respond, "Tom, that makes sense. But it's interesting, because that's the same idea behind God's love for us. It's just like you do with your kids. You don't tolerate their bad or dangerous decisions, but not because you're intolerant. You show them a different way because you care about them and you know what's best for them."

You can't tell how Tom and Gina feel about what your spouse said, so you add, "And they always respond with joy and gratitude that you've shown them a better way." Everyone laughs. Tom adds, "And they just look at us admiringly because we're so wise." More laughter.

### Discuss together:
- How does our motivation affect whether we are perceived as caring or judgmental?
- How did Jesus show people that they needed to change their lives?

> 👤 *Depending on your group, you may want to pause and explore some of the ways that Jesus used parables, questions, and other creative approaches to open people's minds to the idea that he was God.*

6. The mood is now a little lighter, but it's obvious that all four of you are thinking about the conversation. After a minute, Gina looks up and her smile is gone. "But I just don't see how Christians are supposed to be the experts on what God says is best. I trust you two, but I've known Christians who are just bad people. Why should I believe that they know how to explain what's right and wrong?"

You suddenly feel great compassion for Gina because while you don't know the details, you know this question stems from a deeply felt, painful experience in her past. You want to be very careful how you respond. "You're right. I've known some people like that. I've heard some pretty awful stories. I hate it and I wish so badly that those things never happened. But they are misrepresenting who Jesus is and what he stands for. And I believe they've missed the point about what it means to be a Christian."

Seeing that she is listening closely, you continue, "The main role of Christians isn't to tell people how to live. The central message is that God loves you. The part about right and wrong comes in because we can trust his ways are not only right, but good – they show us what's best for us and for the people around us. God's character and God's ways are different from the hurtful Christians you have known, and I believe that Jesus would be angry with those people, and very sad for the people they hurt. Christianity is about God rescuing us, loving us, and giving us a new life."

*Discuss together:*
- How would you explain the Christian basis for morality with those who have had negative experiences with Christians?
- How would you express compassion and love for Gina in a moment like this?

---

7. Tom looks at Gina, who is deep in thought. A few more seconds pass and then Tom lightens the mood. "Ok, that's enough. You almost made my wife cry so we're going to table this discussion and talk about dessert. Chocolate cake for me!" Gina smiles and takes her husband's hand. As the conversation shifts to other topics, you can't help but wonder if you missed another opportunity.

Later that evening, as you're about to go to bed, a text pops up on your phone from Tom. "Thanks for the good conversation tonight." After you write him back, you and your spouse spend some time praying for your friends.

*Discuss together:*

- What's the difference between a real friend and an "evangelistic target"?

---

> *The point of this question is to point out that we shouldn't ever see people as just 'evangelistic targets'. We should approach all people with genuine respect and compassion. Though we want all of our friends to know Christ, we are friends with them regardless of their response.*

- What do you see as the role of prayer in evangelism?

> Consider discussing the significance that these narratives don't necessarily end with your friends appearing to be any closer to faith in Jesus.

## Your Notes:

## Closing Prayer

In his message, Michael said:

> We project an image of ourselves sometimes even at church, sometimes even in our own small group because we want to be accepted whereas what we need to learn is what it means to know what people are really like. Being prepared to be truly open and know the kind of love that comes into our life that is able, both, in its judgment but also in its experience, to reveal who we are and also begin to change us and transform us into all that we should be.

In your discussion, we encourage you to create a safe and accepting environment for everyone to share what they are really like, and to receive the love and support they need to become who God made them to be.

1. Share any updates about your family and friends that your group is praying for.

2. Share any updates on your own life that you would like the group to pray about.

## Weekly Challenge:

A critical part of learning where to start is building genuine friendships with people from different backgrounds and beliefs. Who are some of your favorite people who aren't Christians? This week, do something to continue building your friendship with them. Next week, we will have the opportunity to hear how God worked through these activities.

## For Further Study

If you would like to do additional study on the biblical basis for this week's session, please see the "Next Steps" section at the end of your handbook.

## LEADER OVERVIEW FOR SESSION 7:

If you have the time, you may want to read through the book of Jonah or the crucifixion and resurrection narratives in the Gospels before this week's meeting. Then, think about ways they could be relevant to this conversation with Gina and Tom.

One of the main relational dynamics in this week's story is the many different spiritual perspectives. Gina seems more open, Tom seems resistant, Trevor seems to have a new understanding of the crucifixion, and we aren't sure what Alyssa is thinking. Jonathan and Erica also need to keep their hearts open to what their close friends are thinking as well as what their children are seeing. As the discussion leader, think for a moment about how each of these participants broadens our consideration of what to say—and what not to say—so that everyone is drawn into the conversation.

> **If your schedule permits, set aside some time to pray for each member of your group and the prayer requests they have shared with you.**

At this point in your study, there are probably a number of prayer requests that have been shared in your group. If your schedule permits, set aside some time to pray for each member of your group and the prayer requests they have shared with you.

Before discussing this week's content, we encourage you to review the weekly challenge from last week's session.

³ Beloved, although I was very eager to write to you about our common salvation, I found it necessary to write appealing to you to contend for the faith that was once for all delivered to the saints.
—*Jude 1:3*

# Session 7: Morality

*Morality, Part 2:*
Michael Ramsden

## INTRODUCTION

| | |
|---|---|
| Origin: | Where did everything come from? |
| Meaning: | Why are we here? |
| **Morality:** | **What is right and wrong?** |
| Destiny: | What happens when we die? |

After the intensity of your last dinner conversation, you were very pleasantly surprised when Tom and Gina took you up on the invitation to visit your church for Easter. Afterwards, you and your spouse, your kids Trevor and Alyssa, Tom and Gina, and their two children, all go to lunch together. As everyone is looking through the menu, you notice Trevor just staring blankly at the bottle of ketchup. You ask him, "Trev, are you still with us?" He snaps out of his momentary trance and smiles slightly. "Oh, sorry. I'm here. I was just thinking about what the preacher said the cross was like for Jesus. I don't think I knew how brutal it was until today."

Gina lowers her menu and adds in, "That stood out to me too, Trevor. Actually I was going to ask about that. I found that part of the sermon fascinating. He didn't just talk about what the Bible said, but he really did his research about Roman crucifixion. But still..." she pauses briefly, "Jesus's death is a hard thing to understand – why did God let that happen if he was just going to raise him again a few days later? It doesn't really make sense to me. But I will say I was really surprised by how interesting the sermon was."

It's clear that both Trevor and Gina are genuinely curious about God in a way that they haven't been before. You want to help your son and your next-door neighbor take the next step. At the same time, you know this is a new experience for Tom and Gina, and that Gina had very negative experiences with Christians during her childhood. So where do you start?

*Before starting the video, have a member of your group open your time together in prayer.*

# Video Guide

This guide is intended to make it easy to take notes on Michael's message. The main ideas and quotes are outlined below for your convenience.

### Summary of Session Six:

- God's love and God's judgment are the same in the Old Testament and the New Testament.
- We often confuse justice with vengeance, but they are not the same.
- Love does not exist in the absence of judgment; it exists in the presence of it.
- God knows exactly what we're like and still loves us.
- Love and judgment do not exclude each other; they inform each other.

## Justice and Injustice

### Jonah's anger

*After the repentance and salvation of the people of Nineveh, Jonah is angry at God.*

**Jonah 4:8-9**
But God said to Jonah, "Is it right for you to be angry about the plant?"
"It is," he said. "And I'm so angry I wish I were dead."

*How do we feel when justice collapses?*

**Two Sides of Justice:**
- Question #1: How can I be happy in heaven if God has sent people to hell?
- Question #2: How can I be happy in heaven if the man who sexually abused me as a child is in heaven with me?

*These two questions are linked to the same issue, but they are pulling in very different directions. How do we understand this?*

*When justice collapses in a nation, hope collapses with it.*

**3 Reasons to Punish the Guilty:**
1. To act as a deterrent to other people
2. To rehabilitate, to reform the behavior.
3. To get retribution.

## Justice and Retribution

*If we lose sight of the retributive element of justice, we're in danger of losing justice altogether.*

**CS Lewis, "The Humanitarian Theory of Punishment"** [26]
We demand of a deterrent not whether it is just, but whether it will deter. We demand of a cure not whether it is just, but whether it succeeds. Thus we cease to consider what the criminal deserves and consider only what will cure them or deter others. We have tacitly removed them from the sphere of justice altogether.

*If we drop retribution, we become very confused about how justice operates in any society.*

---

[26] CS Lewis, "The Humanitarian Theory of Punishment" in *Res Judicatae*, 1953.

## Mercy and Justice

*When you extend mercy, you do so at the expense of justice. Instead of getting what you deserve (justice) you get something else (mercy).*

*Does God give up justice in order to be merciful?*

### Jonah 4:2
"...I knew that you are a gracious and compassionate God, slow to anger and abounding in love, a God who relents from sending calamity."

**Compassion:** *to make a moral judgment about something and be moved with passion inside you to do something about it. (If you are not moved to action, you have moralizing.)*

*The God of the Bible looks into every human heart and makes an absolute moral judgment: "That is wrong."*

*And then he is moved in the depths of his being to do something about it. That is the cross.*

*God, in Christ, takes on the full force of all the consequences of sin on the cross; he pays. Justice is met.*

*God doesn't exercise his mercy at the expense of his justice. God exercises his mercy **through** his justice.*

## Justice and Hope

### Isaiah 42:1-4
Here is my servant, whom I uphold, my chosen one in whom I delight; I will put my Spirit on him, and he will bring justice to the nations. He will not shout or cry out, or raise his voice in the streets. A bruised reed he will not break, and a smoldering wick he will not snuff out.
In faithfulness he will bring forth justice;

He will not falter or be discouraged till he establishes justice on earth.
In his teaching the islands will put their hope.

*The consequence of God's justice is hope.*

**A Bruised Reed:** *Tall, thick, and flexible; useless when bruised.*

**A Smoldering Wick:** *From a candle that has burned itself out.*

*Whether you've been crushed through external pressure or you're internally exhausted, God's justice can restore both. God's justice is restorative and it can bring hope.*

*Justice will not fail on that final day.*

**The Bookshelf**

*Who gets into heaven? How good do I have to be?*

*God exercises mercy not at the expense of justice, but through it. That is the basis of all Christian hope regardless of how far from him you may actually be.*

**Summary:**
- As fallen people, we feel a tension both when justice fails and when it succeeds.
- True justice must include the element of retribution.
- God is moved by compassion to exercise his mercy through his justice. The ultimate example of this is Jesus's death on the cross.
- God's justice and mercy working together form the basis for all Christian hope.

> Before going to the small group interaction, you may want to pause and make sure everyone feels comfortable with at least the main points of the lecture.

# Small Group Interaction

Gina's objection to the Easter message was, "Why did God let that happen if He was just going to raise him again a few days later? It doesn't really make sense to me." Though you really want to talk about the cross, you feel paralyzed trying to decide what to say or how to say it.

1. Between your loss for words and your hunger, you find that all you can focus on is whether you should order the cheeseburger or the house salad. Thankfully, as you stare at your menu, your spouse speaks up: "I loved the sermon too. That's one thing I like about our pastor—he doesn't expect us to just take him at his word. He offers evidence and really encourages us to study more on our own. But your question is a good one, and for a long time that didn't really make sense to me either. What I understand about the cross now is that it's about God being both completely just and completely merciful. Jesus receives the punishment appropriate to our sin, which is death; and therefore we can receive mercy, forgiveness, and new life."

*Discuss together:*
- Have you ever found the cross difficult to explain to someone?
- How would you describe the relationship between God's justice and his mercy?

---

*This could be an opportunity to review the lecture if members of your group still have questions. Look back at the notes, and if needed, rewatch parts of the video. Also, if people share that they find the cross difficult to understand or explain, make sure you respond in a way that ensures them that this group is a safe place for sharing and being vulnerable.*

2. There's a pause in the conversation while the waiter takes your order. You notice while everyone is ordering that Tom seems uncomfortable, but he hasn't said anything yet. Gina responds, "Ok, so Jesus receives God's justice so we can be forgiven and go to heaven. But are you saying the suffering and death he endured is what we deserve?"

That strikes a chord with Tom. You hear genuine emotion in his voice as he interjects, "No. I don't buy it. That's not justice, that's more like abuse. I don't deserve that kind of death – no one does. Maybe Hitler or someone really evil. But no one I know. I think most of us are basically good people."

*Discuss together:*
- Have you ever felt like Tom—that Jesus's death on the cross was too severe to be taken as punishment for your own sin?
- How have you heard people express the idea that they are basically a good person?

---

> *You may want to call people's attention to how Jonathan and Erica are picking up on Tom's tone and body language. This is one important way we can notice how people are perceiving and responding to these conversations.*

3. You decide to try and put Tom at ease by sharing your own experience. "I completely understand that Tom. It didn't sound right to me when I first heard it either. But then I thought, 'Either God is really unfair or maybe sin is a bigger deal than I thought.'"

"Or maybe he's just irrational and unpredictable—not someone you can trust," Tom suggests.

"Well, maybe," you reply, "but everything else I know about God suggests that he is loving and kind and fair and consistent and trustworthy. There have also been other things that didn't make sense to me at first, but after learning more I saw them differently. I had every reason to be confident this would make sense too if I looked deeper."

*Discuss together:*
- Have there been areas of the Christian faith that you once found difficult but now make sense to you?
- What might you share with someone to affirm that God is trustworthy and good?

---

*Perhaps you or members of your group can recall ways in which you sometimes find it hard to believe that God is good. Recognizing ways in which we have the same struggles to believe as our nonChristian friends can build empathy and understanding of their perspective.*

4. Trevor is watching you so intently that you turn your head to see if there's a football game on a TV directly behind you. He's not saying anything, but you can tell he's taking it all in. Tom asks another question, but the emotion in his voice seems to have softened. "Ok, so what changed your mind about sin being so awful? What made you see it differently?"

"Well, a lot of things have changed about the way I see sin. Probably the main thing was just putting sin into perspective. I mean, if I lie to you about the size of a fish I caught, the consequences aren't nearly the same as me lying under oath in a court of law. Same act, different consequence. And if I lie to my spouse, there are still different consequences."

You pretend to be avoiding eye contact with your spouse and everyone laughs.

You continue, "So if there were a list of the people it's most serious to offend, God would obviously be at the top of the list, and the consequences of the offense would increase in proportion."

Gina clarifies, "So it's not about the act itself as much as the person being sinned against." You somewhat successfully suppress the sudden surge of enthusiasm and say, "Yes! That's exactly it."

> *This response is not intended to be the 'right' way to explain why sin is serious to someone. It is an approach that may be helpful to some, but make sure to encourage your group to share other possible answers. You may want to be prepared with some yourself.*

### Discuss together:
- What are some other ways you could explain why God takes sin so seriously?
- What are some of the personal and cultural pressures to minimize the reality of sin?

5. Tom really seems to be weighing what you've just said. Gina appears to be thinking, but she doesn't seem to have another question at the moment. You catch your spouse's eye and recognize that neither of you are sure whether to push forward or just leave the conversation there for now.

*Discuss together:*
- How do you decide how much to share? If you have more helpful examples or explanations, how do you evaluate whether to continue or just stop and listen?
- What cues do you look for in others to determine whether to push the conversation forward or leave space for them to decide whether or not to continue?

*One good outcome from this conversation would be for group members to become more comfortable with ambiguity. In most cases, these conversations are not linear progressions from less to more openness to the gospel. If we expect too much out of these discussions, we may become unnecessarily disappointed. Instead, we want to learn to accept people where they are and find graceful ways of helping them take the next step.*

6. Tom looks at your spouse and says, "You've been kind of quiet. Have you wrestled with this question too?"

Your spouse smiles, and appears thankful that Tom wanted to keep talking. "I have—maybe not to the same degree, but it was always helpful to me to ask this question in the bigger context of what I know about God. It's never been a purely intellectual exercise for me. It's really about a relationship with a person—with God. So just like any relationship, you may not always understand, but you make a decision to trust based on what you know of the person. After seeing and experiencing and learning that God was good in so many different ways, I became more willing to trust God in new circumstances or when the Bible taught something that didn't make sense to me at first. Faith isn't a leap in the dark; it is about trusting God in the uncertainties because what we do know about God tells us that he is good and loving."

The conversation continues as Tom and Gina ask more questions, and you both share more about how Jesus has transformed your lives. You're surprised to hear your kids chime in and give examples of how you've changed that you had no idea they had noticed.

As you say goodbye leaving the restaurant, you and your spouse see something in the eyes of both Tom and Gina that you later conclude was a feeling of hopefulness. You spend some more time praying for them as you drive home.

*Discuss together:*
- How would you explain in practical terms, to a non-Christian friend, what it means for your life to be transformed by Jesus?
- As you reflect on Michael's lecture and this lunch conversation, what are the main connections you see between the gospel and discussions about morality?

In next week's session, Dr. John Njoroge, a speaker with Ravi Zacharias International Ministries, will give us a Biblical basis for understanding our destiny.

## Everyday Questions:

As a group, brainstorm some of the "everyday questions" you have heard or might hear on the topic of destiny. Though it may not always be comfortable or appropriate to discuss the topic of our destiny, it is an inevitable part of life. Each week, many people are grieving the death of a famous celebrity, shaken by news of a major disaster (whether natural or man-made), or remembering the anniversary of a significant but troubling event. More personally, the holidays, wedding anniversaries, and birthdays of loved ones who are no longer with us are an often private but nevertheless important way that we are all reminded that this life has an end. Discuss together some of the everyday questions that might lead into a conversation — filled with compassion and hope — on the topic of our morality.

# Your Notes:

# Closing Prayer

Michael said, "Compassion means to make a moral judgment about something and be moved with passion inside you to do something about it." What moral issues are going on in the lives of your family and friends that motivate you to respond with compassion?

1. Share any updates about your family and friends that your group is praying for.

2. Share any updates on your own life that you would like the group to pray about.

## Weekly Challenge:

Part of evangelism is how we pray, how we treat people with respect, and how we share the gospel in a relevant and compassionate way. Another part is how we prepare ourselves for these conversations. Select a topic that needs further study and read at least one article about the subject.

For instance:
- The evidence for the resurrection of Jesus
- Sharing the gospel message using passages from the Bible
- Another topic that has come up in your group discussion

> *One practical way to come alongside your group members is to help them find resources on these topics. Point them to the Next Steps section at the end of the handbook, RZIM.org, or the RZIM YouTube channel.*

## For Further Study

If you would like to do additional study on the biblical basis for this week's session, please see the "Next Steps" section at the end of your handbook.

## LEADER OVERVIEW FOR SESSION 8:

This week's narrative includes a very traumatic story. Just like it "hits home" for Roger, this may be uncomfortably close to real life for some members of your group. As with earlier weeks, it is more important to actually care for one another than to discuss how you might care for other people.

Even if the pain of losing someone in a car accident isn't familiar to your group members, it is the kind of experience that they may unfortunately have to walk through in the future. Either way, an extra degree of sensitivity is in order as you lead the group in this session.

You may also want to discuss how Christians handle grief and tragedy. Deepening our own understanding of how our faith prepares us to walk through these unwanted circumstances can give us a strong foundation for when we need to rely on him the most.

> **As with earlier weeks, it is more important to actually care for one another than to discuss how you might care for other people.**

As in previous weeks, at the start of each session, it is usually a good idea to take the time to catch up with one another. Also, before discussing this week's content, we encourage you to review the weekly challenge from last week's session.

Continue to pray for your group members and for your meeting.

[18] And Jesus came and said to them, "All authority in heaven and on earth has been given to me. [19] Go therefore and make disciples of all nations, baptizing them in[a] the name of the Father and of the Son and of the Holy Spirit, [20] teaching them to observe all that I have commanded you. And behold, I am with you always, to the end of the age."

—Matthew 28:18-20

# Session 8: Destiny

*Destiny, Part 1:*
John Njoroge

**INTRODUCTION**

> Origin: Where did everything come from?
> Meaning: Why are we here?
> Morality: What is right and wrong?
> **Destiny: What happens when we die?**

Right before the last game of Alyssa's all day soccer tournament, your brother Carlos calls with terrible news. His twenty-three-year-old daughter Andrea was just killed in a car accident. You pull your spouse aside and share what happened. Together you step away from the crowd to talk and come up with a plan for what to do next.

You decide that one of you should stay there and let Alyssa finish the game while the other takes Trevor back to the house. Your spouse volunteers to go pack up the car so you can get on the road before dinner. As you look for Trevor, you see the other parents cheering on their girls as the game's opening whistle blows. Roger, whose daughter has been on the same team with Alyssa for the last four years, was watching you instead of the game. You turn away because you don't feel like talking to anyone right now. But he must have seen you on the phone because he looks concerned.

After Trevor and your spouse leave, you find a quiet spot away from the crowd to gather your thoughts. As you look back towards the soccer field, you see Roger walking towards you. As he gets near you start to speak, but tears pour out instead of words. He sits down next to you and you find yourself feeling thankful to have a friend nearby. Finally you take a deep breath and reveal to Roger what happened. You see tears forming in his eyes as he just says, "I'm so deeply sorry." Then he asks, "Is there anything I can do? Can we look after Alyssa? What would help the most?"

Roger's kindness and compassion speak volumes. You say, "Thank you for that. It's very generous of you. But I think I'd like to be here to tell Alyssa as soon as the game is over. She really looked up to her cousin."

Roger asks a few more questions about Andrea, and you tell him you're planning to drive over that night. After a few minutes pass, Roger looks down and says, "My mom died when I was in high school. Drunk driver." Something changed in Roger's voice as he spoke. You hear anger that still sounds fresh, as if the accident had just happened.

Though you don't feel like talking, you have a sense that this could be an important conversation with Roger. But what do you say?

*Before starting the video, have a member of your group open your time together in prayer.*

# Video Guide

This guide is intended to make it easy to take notes on John's message. The main ideas and quotes are outlined below for your convenience.

### Summary of Session Seven:
- As fallen people, we feel a tension both when justice fails and when it succeeds.
- True justice must include the element of retribution.
- God is moved by compassion to exercise his mercy through his justice. The ultimate example of this is Jesus's death on the cross.
- God's justice and mercy working together form the basis for all Christian hope.

## Starting With Wonder

*According to Plato, philosophy is born out of wonder at the questions we all face about our experience:*

- Where did we come from? (Origin)
- Why are we here? (Meaning)
- What is the best way to live? (Morality)
- What happens when we die? (Destiny)

*All worldviews are designed to answer these four questions.*

## Worldview Questions in the Bible

*There isn't much good news in this world. But what does the Bible say to us?*

*We see these four worldview questions in the life of Jesus.*

### John 13:21

> After saying these things, Jesus was troubled in his spirit, and testified, "Truly, truly, I say to you, one of you will betray me."

*Jesus knew the following day would be the worst of his life. He knew, perhaps worst of all, he would experience an abandonment from God the Father.*

*And yet, this same night he chose to wash the feet of the disciples, rather than thinking about himself. Nowhere else in Hebrew or Greek writings do we find a master washing the feet of his students.*

### Jewish Source [27]

> Of all manners of service that a Jewish slave must render to his master, a student must render to his teacher, except that of taking off his shoe.

---

[27] Quoted in Andreas Kostenberger "John", in *Zondervan Illustrated Bible Backgrounds Commentary*, edited by Clinton E. Arnold (Grand Rapid: Zondervan, 2002), 131.

**Jewish Source** [28]
> A Hebrew slave must not wash the feet of his master, nor put his shoes on him.

*How could Jesus be thinking like this, considering the condition he was in?*

*Was Jesus only able to show this love because he was God?*

**John 13:15**
> I have set you an example that you should do as I have done for you.

*Jesus expects you and me to be able to do this kind of thing even in the worst moment of our lives.*

*Throughout history, God's people have served him in the most unimaginable conditions, and they have still excelled in their commitment to who God is.*

**A 19th Century Parisian Ad for Missionaries** [29]
> We offer you no salary, no recompense, no holidays, no pension, but much hard work, a poor dwelling, small consolations, many disappointments, frequent sickness, a violent or lonely death in an unknown grave.

*God's people have served him in the most difficult circumstances in the world.*

---

[28] Quoted in Andreas Kostenberger "John", in *Zondervan Illustrated Bible Backgrounds Commentary*, edited by Clinton E. Arnold (Grand Rapid: Zondervan, 2002), 131.
[29] Quoted in Don Brophy, *The Story of Catholics in America* (Mahwah, NJ: Paulist Press, 1978).

**Poem from a Missionary** [30]
>We the unwilling
>Led by the unknowing
>Are doing the
>Impossible
>For the ungrateful
>
>We have done so much
>For so long
>With so little
>We are now
>Qualified to do anything
>With nothing

*We quickly run out of excuses when we see what God's people have done for him throughout history.*

*How could Jesus and these missionaries do these things? How can it happen for us?*

**John 13:1-5**
>It was just before the Passover Feast. Jesus knew that the time had come for him to leave this world and go to the Father. Having loved his own who were in the world, he now showed them the full extent of his love. The evening meal was being served, and the devil had already prompted Judas Iscariot, son of Simon, to betray Jesus.
>
>Jesus knew that the Father had put all things under his power, and that he had come from God and was returning to God; so he got up from the meal, took off his outer clothing, and wrapped a towel around his waist. After that, he poured water into a basin and began to wash his disciples' feet, drying them with the towel that was wrapped around him.

---

[30] Quoted in Jill Briscoe, *Faith Enough to Finish* (Wheaton, Illinois: Tyndale House Publishers, 2001), 114.

**Three Reasons for Jesus's Actions:**
>Mission: The Father had put all things under his power
>Origin: He had come from God
>Destiny: He was returning to God

## #1: Jesus's Mission

*Jesus knew that God had put all things under his feet.*

*What is your mission in life?*

*Your **life mission** is what you take to be the most important thing about you and why you exist in this world:*
- *What you value (morality)*
- *Why you think you exist (meaning)*

*Why do you exist? (Most people never take the time to ask this.)*

*We all come into this world predisposed to walk away from God.*

*Perhaps one of the worst things that can happen to a human being is that we succeed in something we are pursuing before we have learned to submit to God.*

*The most difficult time to make the right decision is when all the options before us are good ones.*

### Luke 2:48-49
>So when they saw him, they were amazed; and his mother said to him, "Son, why have you done this to us? Look, your father and I have sought you anxiously." And he said to them, "Why did you seek me? Did you not know that I must be about my Father's business?"

*Jesus knew his mission in life, and at the end of his life he knew that it was accomplished.*

## #2: Jesus's Origin

*Jesus knew that he had come from God.*

*Are we here by unguided processes or are we here by divine decree?*

*How we answer the question of origin determines how we deal with each other as human beings.*

**Examples:**
 The genocide in Rwanda in 1994 – "cockroaches"
 The Holocaust – "vermin"
 The unborn – "fetuses"

*How do other worldviews answer this question of origin?*

**Three Categories of Worldviews:**
 1. God doesn't exist. Only the universe exists.
 (Atheism)
 2. Only God exists. The universe doesn't exist.
 (Eastern religions, New Age Movement)
 3. God and the universe exist.
 (Judaism, Christianity, and Islam)

*It is very difficult to sustain the claim that only the universe exists because the universe itself points to the existence of a reality beyond itself—either God or multiple universes.*

**Antony Flew** [31]
> The postulation of multiple universes, I maintained, is a truly desperate alternative. If the existence of one universe requires an explanation, multiple universes require a much bigger explanation: the problem is increased by the factor of whatever the total number of universes is. It seems a little like the case of a schoolboy whose teacher doesn't believe his dog ate his homework, so he replaces the first version with the story that a pack of dogs—too many to count—ate his homework.

*In contrast, the Bible says we are created by God and that puts human beings at a very high level in creation.*

**GK Chesterton** [32]
> The most difficult doctrine to accept in the Scriptures is not the Trinity, the Virgin Birth, or the Incarnation. It is the value that God places on each individual human being.

**Genesis 1:27**
> So God created mankind in his own image,
> in the image of God he created them;
> male and female he created them.

**Psalm 8:4:**
> What is man that you are mindful of him, and the son of man that you care for him?

**Romans 8:29**
> For those God foreknew he also predestined to be conformed to the image of his Son...

---

[31] Antony Flew and Roy Abraham Varghese, *There Is a God: How the World's Most Notorious Atheist Changed His Mind* (New York: HarperOne, 2007), 137.
[32] Quoted in Dallas Willard, *Renovation of the Heart* (Colorado Springs: NavPress, 2002), 46.

**2 Peter 1:4**
> Through these he has given us his very great and precious promises, so that through them you may participate in the divine nature, having escaped the corruption in the world caused by evil desires.

**Revelation 22:5**
> There will be no more night. They will not need the light of a lamp or the light of the sun, for the Lord God will give them light. And they will reign for ever and ever.

*God chose to come in person to rescue us. Jesus's origin, meaning, and morality were all reasons why he could serve his disciples in the most difficult moment of his life.*

**Summary:**
- All worldviews should answer the four questions of origins, meaning, morality, and destiny.
- Jesus's life mission was that God had put all things under his feet. Our life mission and meaning can only come from God.
- Jesus's origin was that God sent him. Our origin of being made in God's image gives us great inherent value and a standard for moral treatment of each other.
- If we understand our origin, life mission, and destiny, we can serve God even in the most difficult moments of our lives.

> *Before going to the small group interaction, you may want to pause and make sure everyone feels comfortable with at least the main points of the lecture.*

# Small Group Interaction

1. Roger has just revealed to you that he lost his mother when he was in high school, and you can tell that it's something he still finds very painful. You're feeling intense grief yourself, but you believe that this is an opportunity God is giving you to serve your friend.

> *It should be clear that this sense that God is prompting you to speak to Roger should not be out of a sense of guilt, but out of the knowledge that God can often use unexpected situations to lead to life changing moments or conversations.*

*Discuss together:*
- In John's lecture, he discussed how Jesus was able to serve his disciples in the midst of extremely difficult circumstances. How would you feel about talking with a friend in a situation like this?
- How has your faith helped you through tragedy in the past? In what ways do you sense that your faith has prepared you for unexpected losses that may come in the future?

---
---
---
---

2. You take a deep breath and ask God to give you wisdom and strength. But you also wonder at the timing of this conversation. Now seems like the worst possible time for you to have to talk about faith. You find yourself resisting your own anger towards God for letting Andrea die. In the midst of your own sadness, tears come again as you tell him how sorry you are about his loss. A minute or two goes by, and then you ask, "So how did you deal with it?"

Roger shakes his head, "I didn't, really. Time, maybe? But it still hurts a lot. My only advice is to not ask the 'why' questions. They will drive you crazy because there are no answers. Love the ones you still have. Be there for people who need you. That's all I've got."

A minute passes while you think about what to say. You decide to be honest about what you're feeling. "I'm angry right now. I was trying to pray before, but part of me doesn't want to. I'm just mad at God. Maybe I shouldn't be, but that's what I feel."

***Discuss together:***
- What do you think about sharing with someone who doesn't believe in God that you are angry with him or have doubts?
- How have you seen your non-Christian friends respond to the loss of loved ones?

---
---
---
---
---

3. Roger says, "Yeah, when it happened my Dad tried to take me to a Christian counselor, but we just didn't connect. Nothing he said could ever make it okay that my Mom was gone. So, I don't know. But... you find prayer helpful? Has it helped you through something like this before?"

Looking at the soccer game, you think about Roger's question. At first, nothing comes to mind. Then you start to think about what you've heard people say, but you're held back by a fear that in the middle of your current grief you won't sound convincing. Feeling uncertain about what to do, you silently pray that the Holy Spirit would give you words.

Finally, you say, "No, this is new for me. I became a Christian five years ago, so I'm just starting to figure this out. I know that God is good and that he answers prayers. So as hard as it is, I trust that he's going to be with me through this too."

*Discuss together:*
- What are some of the ways that answers and explanations can make things worse?
- How have you experienced God's presence in your own life?

---
---
---
---

4. Roger takes a moment to consider what you've shared. He looks genuinely perplexed as he asks, "But even with this… why do you still trust him? I mean, I'm not trying to change your mind. I just see things differently and I wonder why someone would believe in a God who allows bad things to happen when he could stop them."

"That's a great question," you reply, not yet sure how to answer. "I do trust him. I think maybe right now I have to lean on the things I know in my head even if I don't feel them in my heart. I know God is real, and he is good. I know God doesn't like to see us in pain." Suddenly the story of Lazarus comes to mind. "There's a story in the Bible of when Jesus learned that his friend Lazarus had died. Even though Jesus was about to raise him from the dead, he still wept when he got to the tomb—I think because he saw people he cared about who were really hurting."

It appears Roger is taking in what you're saying, but he doesn't reply. You continue, "So I don't know why God let Andrea die. I don't know why your Mom was in that accident." The immensity of your loss surges and the tears come again. You pause for a moment, but then keep going. "But I know that if God has a reason, even if I don't ever know what it is, I can trust that it's a good reason."

*Discuss together:*
- How do you understand God's response to suffering?
- How do we continue to trust God in situations where we can't make sense of what we are experiencing?

_____

_____

_____

_____

5. Roger slowly nods his head and replies, "I've never really thought about it like that. Before I decided he didn't exist, I kind of had this idea that God is this distant, perfect, old man in the clouds. It's really hard to believe that I would actually matter to God."

You're about to say more when your phone rings. It's your spouse saying the car is ready and wanting to know how much time was left in the game. You realize that the game must be almost over and you have missed nearly all of it talking to Roger. You update your spouse and say you'll have Alyssa ready and waiting when they arrive. You ask how Trevor is doing. "He's just been really quiet," you're told.

As you put away your phone you look at Roger. You know that in a few minutes you need to go to Alyssa and break the news, so you probably need to wrap up the conversation.

*Discuss together:*
- If you only had a few minutes left in this conversation, what would you say?

- How does taking a long-term perspective affect your approach to evangelism?

## Your Notes:

## Closing Prayer

1. Share any updates about your family and friends that your group is praying for.

2. Share any updates on your own life that you would like the group to pray about.

## Weekly Challenge:

In John's lecture, he said "We quickly run out of excuses when we see what God's people have done for him throughout history." Because of what Jesus has done for us, our destiny is secure. Discuss with your group how you want to move forward this week in loving and serving those around you.

## For Further Study

If you would like to do additional study on the biblical basis for this week's session, please see the "Next Steps" section at the end of your handbook.

## LEADER OVERVIEW FOR SESSION 9:

This lesson will create an opportunity for members of your group to think through how they might respond to individuals in their lives who are similar to the characters presented here in the narrative. There are no new characters introduced here, but this lesson creates an opportunity to engage with each person described so far in the study. Your group members will be allowed to choose one of the characters and imagine how a conversation might go with them if they continued the discussion beyond what is presented in this week's narrative.

❗ **The reality is that today millions of people regularly share very personal thoughts online, and in many cases it can lead to opportunities to discuss life's bigger questions.**

The central event of the story this week is your posting of a comment about Andrea to social media. You wanted to share with your friends what Andrea meant to you and how you've felt personally challenged since her death. Some of your group members may feel that this is not something they would feel comfortable doing. That's completely fine. The reality is that today millions of people regularly share very personal thoughts online, and in many cases it can lead to opportunities to discuss life's bigger questions.

In this case, it does lead to opportunities to further engage with friends and family members who respond to the post. The main goal is to focus on the conversations with friends and family members, not whether we use social media in this particular way. As a way of wrapping up this nine week study, we want to create an opportunity for group members to think through how future conversations might develop. Ultimately this should be a helpful exercise in preparing for future interaction with real individuals they know and care about and would love to see know Christ.

> **❗ Ultimately this should be a helpful exercise in preparing for future interaction with real individuals they know and care about and would love to see know Christ.**

At the end of the session, your group will be asked to write down how they might share the gospel with one of the characters in the story. This can be an extremely helpful and important exercise for those who don't feel comfortable sharing the gospel, and even for those who do. Make sure there's time for this question before you wrap up.

Before discussing this week's content, we encourage you to review the weekly challenge from last week's session.

Continue to pray for your group members and for your meeting.

# Session 9: Destiny

*Destiny, Part 2:*
John Njoroge

## INTRODUCTION

| | |
|---|---|
| Origin: | Where did everything come from? |
| Meaning: | Why are we here? |
| Morality: | What is right and wrong? |
| **Destiny:** | **What happens when we die?** |

A couple weeks have gone by since your niece Andrea passed away in a tragic car accident. Her name still comes up almost daily within your family as you all grieve the loss. Trevor and Alyssa have had some questions. You've had a few of your own. The significance of being able to openly discuss these questions together as a family is not lost on you. Over dinner one night you find yourself talking about how much you admired your niece and that you wished the world could know how special she was.

Your son Trevor has a suggestion. "Hey, you should post something online. What you just said would be perfect." So after dinner, you share your thoughts on a social network:

> Hey everyone,
>
> Just over two weeks ago our family lost someone very special. My niece Andrea was a remarkable individual. She was only 22, but someone I greatly admired. She was smart, beautiful, respectful, honest and kind. She babysat Trevor and Alyssa and never let us pay her—ever. When God made her, he made someone exceptional. And I have no idea why he let her go so soon.
>
> I don't know if Andrea knew how much we all thought of her. I hope it was clear from how we treated her. But I don't know if we ever told her. If I could redo anything, I wouldn't have assumed she knew how we felt. I so wish that I had told her how much her example meant to me.

One of the ways that Andrea touched my own life the most was how she loved God. I know that Carlos and Amy set an incredible example for her in how they raised her. When I was skeptical about religion, Andrea's own example of following Jesus kept me open to the possibility that God was there.

I don't know if Andrea knew how remarkable she was, but I want the world to know, so I'm posting it here. Her life was beautiful for so many reasons, but the brightest light of her life came, I believe, from Jesus. That was the message Andrea shared and in honor of her I want to share it more boldly too. Because it's true for everyone who reads this. God delights in you because he made you. And I'd love to tell you more about that.

After you hit the "share" button, you feel some anxiety about what people might think. You bow your head in prayer, asking God to continue to be near to you as you grieve Andrea's death and to give you more opportunities to share about his love with your family and friends.

*Before starting the video, have a member of your group open your time together in prayer.*

# Video Guide

This guide is intended to make it easy to take notes on John's message. The main ideas and quotes are outlined below for your convenience.

### *Summary of Session Eight:*
- All worldviews should answer the four questions of origins, meaning, morality, and destiny.
- Jesus's life mission was that God had put all things under his feet. Our life mission and meaning can only come from God.

- Jesus's origin was that God sent him. Our origin of being made in God's image gives us great inherent value and a standard for moral treatment of each other.
- If we understand our origin, life mission, and destiny, we can serve God even in the most difficult moments of our lives.

## #3: Jesus's Destiny

*Jesus's mission in life was very clearly defined and he followed it to the end.*

### John 13:3
"He knew that he was going to God."

## Destiny in Atheism

*What happens to us when we die?*

### Bertrand Russell, "A Free Man's Worship" [33]

> That Man is the product of causes which had no prevision of the end they were achieving; that his origin, his growth, his hopes and fears, his loves and his beliefs, are but the outcome of accidental collocations of atoms; that no fire, no heroism, no intensity of thought and feeling, can preserve an individual life beyond the grave; that all the labours of the ages, all the devotion, all the inspiration, all the noonday brightness of human genius, are destined to extinction in the vast death of the solar system, and that the whole temple of Man's achievement must inevitably be buried beneath the débris of a universe in ruins—all these things, if not quite beyond dispute, are yet so nearly certain, that no philosophy which rejects them can hope to stand. Only within the scaffolding of these truths, only on the firm foundation of unyielding despair, can the soul's habitation henceforth be safely built.

---

[33] Bertrand Russell, *Mysticism and Logic: And Other Essays* (London: Longmans, Green & Co, 1919), 47-48.

*You have to come to terms with the fact that nothing you do in this world will matter in the end.*

**Three Categories of Worldview:**
1. God doesn't exist. Only the universe exists. (Atheism)
2. Only God exists. The universe doesn't exist. (Eastern religions, New Age Movement)
3. God and the universe exist. (Judaism, Christianity, and Islam)

## Destiny in Eastern Religions

*These religions tell you nothing happens to you when you die because you never existed.*

*The problem is: in order to deny your own existence, you have to exist.*

## Destiny in the Bible

**Acts 7:56, 59**
> "Look," he said, "I see heaven open and the Son of Man standing at the right hand of God."
>
> While they were stoning him, Stephen prayed, "Lord Jesus, receive my spirit."

*We are souls and spirits, not just physical beings. When we die, we don't cease to exist; we exist in the presence of God at that very moment of death.*

**1 Thessalonians 4:13**
> Brothers, we do not want you to be ignorant about those who fall asleep, or to grieve like the rest of men, who have no hope.

*We will have physical bodies when Jesus comes back. All of creation is valuable to God.*

## Jesus's Eternal Perspective

**John 13:1**
> Jesus knew that the hour had come for him to leave this world and go to the Father.

*Jesus was not overtaken by events taking place around him; he lived with an eternal perspective, in tune with God.*

*When we live like that, it becomes easy to trust God even when he seems silent in our lives.*

*There will come a time when you're going to have to depend on what you know to be true. The time to be grounded in these ideas is now; not when you are going through those experiences.*

**John 17:3**
> Now this is eternal life: that they know you, the only true God, and Jesus Christ, whom you have sent.

*Eternal life is knowing God through Jesus and it begins the moment we believe.*

*We are going to live forever – but not in this world, and not in this condition.*

*What does this all mean for you and for me? What does it look like in our lives?*

## #1: We Are Not Our Own

*We were bought for a price. We are here for a purpose. We are accountable to God.*

### John 3:16-18
For God so loved the world that he gave his one and only Son, that whoever believes in him shall not perish but have eternal life. For God did not send his Son into the world to condemn the world, but to save the world through him. Whoever believes in him is not condemned, but whoever does not believe stands condemned already because they have not believed in the name of God's one and only Son.

### William Cowper, "There Is a Fountain Filled with Blood"
There is a fountain filled with blood drawn from Emmanuel's veins;
And sinners plunged beneath that flood lose all their guilty stains.

## #2: Our Identity Is Secure

*It is very hard for us to be who we truly are before other people, because sometimes even we don't know who we really are.*

*The Bible teaches that all of us are truly priceless. All the ways we classify and value people will amount to nothing when we stand before God.*

## #3: We Can Live in Freedom

*For many people to be free is to do what you want, when you want to do it, and how you want to do it.*

*What does it mean to be free?*

**John 8:31-32**
> To the Jews who had believed him, Jesus said, "If you hold to my teaching, you are really my disciples. Then you will know the truth, and the truth will set you free."

*Freedom is the ability to function the way God designed you to function.*

*Our destiny becomes the guiding principle in all that we do.*

*We are not home yet.*

**Malcolm Muggeridge, "But Not of Christ"** [34]
> In Christian terms, such hopes and fears are equally beside the point. As Christians we know that here we have no continuing city, that crowns roll in the dust and every earthly kingdom must sometime flounder, whereas we acknowledge a king men did not crown and cannot dethrone, as we are citizens of a city of God they did not build and cannot destroy.

**Summary:**
- Atheist worldviews say that when we die, we cease to exist; we have to accept that nothing we do has ultimate meaning in the end.
- Eastern religions say that nothing happens to us when we die because we never existed to begin with.
- The Bible says that when we die, we do not cease to exist — we exist in the presence of God at that very moment of death.
- Because he had an eternal perspective, Jesus was able to minister to those around him even in the worst moment of his life.
- As Christians we share Jesus's eternal perspective: we are not our own, our identity is secure, and we can live in freedom.

---

[34] *Seeing Through the Eye: Malcolm Muggeridge on Faith*, ed. Cecil Kuhne (San Francisco: Ignatius Press, 2005).

> **Before going to the small group interaction, you may want to pause and make sure everyone feels comfortable with at least the main points of the lecture.**

# Small Group Interaction

About twenty minutes after you post your tribute to Andrea, Trevor comes to find you and says, "Lots of people liked what you wrote! I just logged in to share your post on my profile and saw that tons of people have read it and shared it too."

You open your computer and log back in to see the positive feedback. Several people have left comments, including your brother. He simply wrote, "Thank you for this. It's beautiful." You're surprised by how quickly people have responded to your post. You read a few more comments and then see that there are two private messages waiting.

The first one is from Fred:
> Hey, I remember you mentioning Andrea a few times. I'm really sorry for your loss. Your post got me thinking. The treatment plan for my cancer starts next week and I'm worried about what happens if it doesn't work out. I mean, I prayed with you, but how do I know if, you know, everything is good with God? Let's talk soon.

Feeling encouraged, you reply and ask Fred if he's free for lunch the next day. Then you open the next one. It's from Uncle Bob, and it quickly brings you back down to earth. His anger is just as clear when he writes as when he speaks:

Why did you have to do that? Your post was great until you brought God into it. You really have to make everything about your made up religion don't you? Using this tragedy to "share the good news"? Give me a break. Sad. So, so, so sad. Your religion has made you a real jerk, you know that?

Trevor looks at you and says, "Wow, that's kind of harsh." You nod your head in agreement and decide to postpone writing back. "I'll have to write him back later," you tell Trevor. "I want to be really careful with how I reply."

Trevor looks like he wants to ask a question, but he doesn't say anything. You close the laptop and focus on your son. "Trevor, what's on your mind?"

He takes a second, then opens up, "I've been thinking a lot about what you've been saying and it is starting to make sense to me. But I still have some questions. I mean, I know it is comforting to think that Andrea is in heaven now, but how do we know that's really where she is?"

You say, "Trevor, that's a really great question. Let's think about it together, ok?"

***Discuss together:***
- This week's discussion will be different from the others. We want you to script a conversation with Fred, Uncle Bob, or Trevor. For the next five to ten minutes, take some time to write out your own best case scenario for how these conversations might go. You could also create your own scenario with someone you expect to talk with in the near future about God. Think about what you would say, but also try your best to imagine how they are most likely to respond. After you have

had the opportunity to think about how you would imagine these conversations going, come back together and share your scenarios with one another.

*This may be difficult for some group members. If it's helpful, have them work in pairs based on the character they'd like to address. Also, to clarify, each person/pair is to work on one conversation each, not all of them.*

- For the next part, take another five to ten minutes to write out how you would share the gospel in one of these conversations. Then come back together again to share with one another what you've written.

> **This is really important.** Do the members of your group know how they would explain the gospel to someone? An exercise that requires them to actually put it into words can be extremely helpful, so make sure you leave time for this.

- Finally, as you come to the end of *Everyday Questions*, share with your group the main ideas, principles, or other takeaways that you've learned during these sessions.

## Your Notes:

## Closing Prayer

1. Share any updates about your family and friends that your group is praying for.

2. Share any updates on your own life that you would like the group to pray about.

## Weekly Challenge:

Congratulations! Now that you've finished *Everyday Questions*, it is time to make a plan to keep growing in your faith and sharing about Jesus with others. RZIM stands ready to come alongside you. Here are some options to look into:

- The RZIM Academy (www.rzimacademy.org)
- The RZIM Speaking Team (http://rzim.org/teams)
- The RZIM Media Resources (http://rzim.org/media)
- The "Next Steps" section in your handbook

# Next Steps: Bible Studies

## WEEK 1: INTRODUCTION

*1 Peter 3:8-18*

[8] Finally, all of you, have unity of mind, sympathy, brotherly love, a tender heart, and a humble mind. [9] Do not repay evil for evil or reviling for reviling, but on the contrary, bless, for to this you were called, that you may obtain a blessing. [10] For

> "Whoever desires to love life
> and see good days,
> let him keep his tongue from evil
> and his lips from speaking deceit;
> [11] let him turn away from evil and do good;
> let him seek peace and pursue it.
> [12] For the eyes of the Lord are on the righteous,
> and his ears are open to their prayer.
> But the face of the Lord is against those who do evil."

[13] Now who is there to harm you if you are zealous for what is good? [14] But even if you should suffer for righteousness' sake, you will be blessed. Have no fear of them, nor be troubled, [15] but in your hearts honor Christ the Lord as holy, always being prepared to make a defense to anyone who asks you for a reason for the hope that is in you; yet do it with gentleness and respect, [16] having a good conscience, so that, when you are slandered, those who revile your good behavior in Christ may be put to shame. [17] For it is better to suffer for doing good, if that should be God's will, than for doing evil.

*Study Questions for 1 Peter 3:8-18*

*Begin your study with a moment of prayer.*
*Ask God to open your heart and mind as you study his word.*

1. Review the passage and list the commands that Peter gives to the recipients of his letter.

2. What encouragement does Peter give to Christians who experience suffering?

3. Reflect on verse 12. What does it mean that "the eyes of the Lord" are on the righteous?

4. Peter assumes that obedience to this way of life will lead people to ask these Christians to provide 'a reason for the hope that is in you' (vv. 14-15).
What is our hope?

How are you prepared to explain the reasons for your hope in Christ?

5. In verse eight, Peter encourages his readers to embrace five virtues: unity of mind, sympathy, brotherly love, a tender heart, and a humble mind. As you begin this study on evangelism, how can you intentionally cultivate these character traits in your life?

# WEEK 2: ORIGIN

*Genesis 1:26-31*

26 Then God said, "Let us make man in our image, after our likeness. And let them have dominion over the fish of the sea and over the birds of the heavens and over the livestock and over all the earth and over every creeping thing that creeps on the earth."
27      So God created man in his own image,
         in the image of God he created him;
            male and female he created them.
28 And God blessed them. And God said to them, "Be fruitful and multiply and fill the earth and subdue it, and have dominion over the fish of the sea and over the birds of the heavens and over every living thing that moves on the earth." 29 And God said, "Behold, I have given you every plant yielding seed that is on the face of all the earth, and every tree with seed in its fruit. You shall have them for food. 30 And to every beast of the earth and to every bird of the heavens and to everything that creeps on the earth, everything that has the breath of life, I have given every green plant for food." And it was so. 31 And God saw everything that he had made, and behold, it was very good. And there was evening and there was morning, the sixth day.

## Study Questions for Genesis 1:26-31

*Begin your study with a moment of prayer.*
*Ask God to open your heart and mind as you study his word.*

1. In Genesis 1, the authority on human identity and value is God. "God said..."
Who are some of the alternative authorities on human identity and value?
How do they define human life?

2. In this passage, what responsibilities does God give to us?

3. How does being made in God's image help shape your own self-perception?

4. In verse 31, we notice that God surveys his creation and declares it 'very good'. In days one through five, the evaluation of the Creation is simply 'good.' What significance does this change in emphasis have for our understanding of human origins?

5. What can you do to demonstrate that you believe every human being is made in God's image?

## Background notes:
- "Ancient oriental kings were often seen as bearing the image of their god, but Genesis affirms that every human being is made in God's image" (New Bible Commentary).

# WEEK 3: ORIGIN

## Colossians 1:15-23

[15] [Jesus] is the image of the invisible God, the firstborn of all creation. [16] For by him all things were created, in heaven and on earth, visible and invisible, whether thrones or dominions or rulers or authorities—all things were created through him and for him. [17] And he is before all things, and in him all things hold together. [18] And he is the head of the body, the church. He is the beginning, the firstborn from the dead, that in everything he might be preeminent. [19] For in him all the fullness of God was pleased to dwell, [20] and through him to reconcile to himself all things, whether on earth or in heaven, making peace by the blood of his cross.

[21] And you, who once were alienated and hostile in mind, doing evil deeds, [22] he has now reconciled in his body of flesh by his death, in order to present you holy and blameless and above reproach before him, [23] if indeed you continue in the faith, stable and steadfast, not shifting from the hope of the gospel that you heard, which has been proclaimed in all creation under heaven, and of which I, Paul, became a minister.

## Study Questions for Colossians 1:15-23

*Begin your study with a moment of prayer.*
*Ask God to open your heart and mind as you study his word.*

1. List the ways this passage demonstrates the supreme glory of Jesus:

2. Verse 16 teaches that all things were "created through him and for him." How does being created by God and for God affect how we value human beings?

3. Verse 21 boldly states we were "alienated and hostile in mind, doing evil deeds." In what ways has sin impacted your view of human value? Think of how you view others as well as how you view yourself.

4. Paul states that Christ has reconciled us to one another (verse 22). To whom might you need to be reconciled in your church?

5. Paul urges his readers to "continue in the faith, stable and steadfast, not shifting from the hope of the gospel." How can you personally apply this teaching?

### Background notes:
- "In the OT 'firstborn' occurs 130 times to describe one who is supreme or first in time. It also refers to one who had a special place in the father's love: so 'Israel is my firstborn son' (Ex. 4:22)" (New Bible Commentary).
- Comment on Colossians 1:18: "Christ is the beginning in the sense that he is the firstborn from among the dead, i.e. the founder of a new humanity" (New Bible Commentary).

# WEEK 4: MEANING

*Romans 8:18-25*

[18] For I consider that the sufferings of this present time are not worth comparing with the glory that is to be revealed to us. [19] For the creation waits with eager longing for the revealing of the sons of God. [20] For the creation was subjected to futility, not willingly, but because of him who subjected it, in hope [21] that the creation itself will be set free from its bondage to corruption and obtain the freedom of the glory of the children of God. [22] For we know that the whole creation has been groaning together in the pains of childbirth until now. [23] And not only the creation, but we ourselves, who have the firstfruits of the Spirit, groan inwardly as we wait eagerly for adoption as sons, the redemption of our bodies. [24] For in this hope we were saved. Now hope that is seen is not hope. For who hopes for what he sees? [25] But if we hope for what we do not see, we await for it with patience.

## Study Questions for Romans 8:18-25

*Begin your study with a moment of prayer.*
*Ask God to open your heart and mind as you study his word.*

In these eight verses Paul recaps the major chapters of the Christian story: a good creation, subjected to futility, hoping for redemption.

1. List the ways this passage explains the unique hope of the Christian worldview:

2. How does the fall - including 'the sufferings of this present time' (verse 18) - affect how we perceive the meaning of our lives?

3. What connections does Paul make between the creation and God's children?

4. What sufferings have you experienced—or are you experiencing—that make it difficult to trust that God will one day bring redemption?

5. Write a prayer to God expressing your hope in the fulfillment of his plan:

### Background notes:
- "In the OT, 'glory' denotes the 'weight' and majesty of God's presence" (New Bible Commentary).

# WEEK 5: MEANING

*Ecclesiastes 1:1-14*

¹ The words of the Preacher, the son of David, king in Jerusalem.
²     Vanity of vanities, says the Preacher,
        vanity of vanities! All is vanity.
³     What does man gain by all the toil
        at which he toils under the sun?
⁴     A generation goes, and a generation comes,
        but the earth remains forever.
⁵     The sun rises, and the sun goes down,
        and hastens to the place where it rises.
⁶     The wind blows to the south
        and goes around to the north;
    around and around goes the wind,
        and on its circuits the wind returns.
⁷     All streams run to the sea,
        but the sea is not full;
    to the place where the streams flow,
        there they flow again.
⁸     All things are full of weariness;
        a man cannot utter it;
    the eye is not satisfied with seeing,
        nor the ear filled with hearing.
⁹     What has been is what will be,
        and what has been done is what will be done,
        and there is nothing new under the sun.
¹⁰    Is there a thing of which it is said,
        "See, this is new"?
   It has been already
       in the ages before us.
¹¹    There is no remembrance of former things,
        nor will there be any remembrance
   of later things yet to be
       among those who come after.

¹² I the Preacher have been king over Israel in Jerusalem. ¹³ And I applied my heart to seek and to search out by wisdom all that is done under heaven. It is an unhappy business that God has given to the children of man to be busy with. ¹⁴ I have seen everything that is done under the sun, and behold, all is vanity and a striving after wind.

### Study Questions for Ecclesiastes 1:1-14

*Begin your study with a moment of prayer.*
*Ask God to open your heart and mind as you study his word.*

1. What are the examples from how the natural world works in this chapter of Ecclesiastes? What point is "the Preacher" emphasizing by listing so many examples?

2. What are some modern day examples of the vanity and meaninglessness of life?

3. The author of Ecclesiastes intends the answer to the question of verse 3, "What does man gain by all the toil at which he toils under the sun?" to be 'nothing'. If you're really honest with yourself, how might you answer this question?

4. What are some of the ways you see your family and friends expressing a desire for life to be more than a "vanity of vanities"?

5. What is your reaction when you see people who are preoccupied with "a striving after wind" (verse 14)? Take some time to pray for these people. Pray also that you would respond to them with compassion.

### Background notes:
- "Under the sun" is often understood as referring to all of human activity without reference to God.

# WEEK 6: MORALITY

*Jonah 4:1-11*

¹ But it displeased Jonah exceedingly and he was angry. ² And he prayed to the LORD and said, "O LORD, is not this what I said when I was yet in my country? That is why I made haste to flee to Tarshish; for I knew that you are a gracious God and merciful, slow to anger and abounding in steadfast love, and relenting from disaster. ³ Therefore now, O LORD, please take my life from me, for it is better for me to die than to live." ⁴ And the LORD said, "Do you do well to be angry?"
⁵ Jonah went out of the city and sat to the east of the city and made a booth for himself there. He sat under it in the shade, till he should see what would become of the city. ⁶ Now the LORD God appointed a plant and made it come up over Jonah, that it might be a shade over his head, to save him from his discomfort. So Jonah was exceedingly glad because of the plant. ⁷ But when dawn came up the next day, God appointed a worm that attacked the plant, so that it withered. ⁸ When the sun rose, God appointed a scorching east wind, and the sun beat down on the head of Jonah so that he was faint. And he asked that he might die and said, "It is better for me to die than to live." ⁹ But God said to Jonah, "Do you do well to be angry for the plant?" And he said, "Yes, I do well to be angry, angry enough to die." ¹⁰ And the LORD said, "You pity the plant, for which you did not labor, nor did you make it grow, which came into being in a night and perished in a night. ¹¹ And should not I pity Nineveh, that great city, in which there are more than 120,000 persons who do not know their right hand from their left, and also much cattle?"

## *Study Questions for Jonah 4:1-11*

*Begin your study with a moment of prayer.*
*Ask God to open your heart and mind as you study his word.*

1. In this passage, what makes Jonah angry? What makes him happy?

2. Describe what Jonah believes God ought to do.

3. In Jonah 4, God teaches Jonah a very important lesson about his power and mercy. How does God teach Jonah this lesson?

4. What does this passage teach us about God's character and purposes?

5. The book of Jonah emphasizes God's love for both his reluctant prophet and a rebellious city. At the same time, it reveals the difficulty of accepting that God loves people we would consider to be our enemies. Who might God be asking you to love?

# WEEK 7: MORALITY

*Romans 5:6-21*

⁶ For while we were still weak, at the right time Christ died for the ungodly. ⁷ For one will scarcely die for a righteous person—though perhaps for a good person one would dare even to die— ⁸ but God shows his love for us in that while we were still sinners, Christ died for us. ⁹ Since, therefore, we have now been justified by his blood, much more shall we be saved by him from the wrath of God. ¹⁰ For if while we were enemies we were reconciled to God by the death of his Son, much more, now that we are reconciled, shall we be saved by his life. ¹¹ More than that, we also rejoice in God through our Lord Jesus Christ, through whom we have now received reconciliation.
¹² Therefore, just as sin came into the world through one man, and death through sin, and so death spread to all men because we all sinned— ¹³ for sin indeed was in the world before the law was given, but sin is not counted where there is no law. ¹⁴ Yet death reigned from Adam to Moses, even over those whose sinning was not like the transgression of Adam, who was a type of the one who was to come.
¹⁵ But the free gift is not like the trespass. For if many died through one man's trespass, much more have the grace of God and the free gift by the grace of that one man Jesus Christ abounded for many. ¹⁶ And the free gift is not like the result of that one man's sin. For the judgment following one trespass brought condemnation, but the free gift following many trespasses brought justification. ¹⁷ For if, because of one man's trespass, death reigned through that one man, much more will those who receive the abundance of grace and the free gift of righteousness reign in life through the one man Jesus Christ.
¹⁸ Therefore, as one trespass led to condemnation for all men, so one act of righteousness leads to justification and life for all men. ¹⁹ For as by the one man's disobedience the many were made sinners, so by the one man's obedience the many will be made righteous. ²⁰ Now the law came in to increase the trespass, but where sin increased, grace abounded all the more, ²¹ so that, as sin reigned in death, grace also might reign through righteousness leading to eternal life through Jesus Christ our Lord.

## Study Questions for Romans 5:6-21

*Begin your study with a moment of prayer.*
*Ask God to open your heart and mind as you study his word.*

1. In this passage, Paul repeatedly contrasts Adam and Jesus. List the contrasts.

| Adam | Jesus |
|---|---|
|  |  |
|  |  |
|  |  |
|  |  |
|  |  |
|  |  |

2. When you think about or discuss the gospel, do you tend to emphasize either 'justice' or 'mercy' at the expense of the other?

3. In your own words, write a summary of this passage.

4. How does this passage encourage us to be humble?

5. Given what God has done for you, how can you show God's love to your family and friends?

# WEEK 8: DESTINY

*John 13:1-20*

¹ Now before the Feast of the Passover, when Jesus knew that his hour had come to depart out of this world to the Father, having loved his own who were in the world, he loved them to the end. ² During supper, when the devil had already put it into the heart of Judas Iscariot, Simon's son, to betray him, ³ Jesus, knowing that the Father had given all things into his hands, and that he had come from God and was going back to God, ⁴ rose from supper. He laid aside his outer garments, and taking a towel, tied it around his waist. ⁵ Then he poured water into a basin and began to wash the disciples' feet and to wipe them with the towel that was wrapped around him. ⁶ He came to Simon Peter, who said to him, "Lord, do you wash my feet?" ⁷ Jesus answered him, "What I am doing you do not understand now, but afterward you will understand." ⁸ Peter said to him, "You shall never wash my feet." Jesus answered him, "If I do not wash you, you have no share with me." ⁹ Simon Peter said to him, "Lord, not my feet only but also my hands and my head!" ¹⁰ Jesus said to him, "The one who has bathed does not need to wash, except for his feet, but is completely clean. And you are clean, but not every one of you." ¹¹ For he knew who was to betray him; that was why he said, "Not all of you are clean." ¹² When he had washed their feet and put on his outer garments and resumed his place, he said to them, "Do you understand what I have done to you? ¹³ You call me Teacher and Lord, and you are right, for so I am. ¹⁴ If I then, your Lord and Teacher, have washed your feet, you also ought to wash one another's feet. ¹⁵ For I have given you an example, that you also should do just as I have done to you. ¹⁶ Truly, truly, I say to you, a servant is not greater than his master, nor is a messenger greater than the one who sent him. ¹⁷ If you know these things, blessed are you if you do them. ¹⁸ I am not speaking of all of you; I know whom I have chosen. But the Scripture will be fulfilled, 'He who ate my bread has lifted his heel against me.' ¹⁹ I am telling you this now, before it takes place, that when it does take place you may believe that I am he. ²⁰ Truly, truly, I say to you, whoever receives the one I send receives me, and whoever receives me receives the one who sent me."

## Study Questions for John 13:1-20

*Begin your study with a moment of prayer.*
*Ask God to open your heart and mind as you study his word.*

1. Study the passage for insights into Jesus' self-understanding. How does he view himself?

2. How would you feel if Jesus asked to wash your feet?

3. In this passage, there are a few reminders that Judas will betray Jesus (verses 2, 11, 18). Still, Jesus washes his feet too. What does Jesus teach us by washing the feet of Judas?

4. Jesus promises that we will be blessed if we follow his example (verse 17). Take a moment to remember God's faithfulness to you. How has he blessed your obedience to his will?

5. Ask God to give you wisdom on whom to serve and how to serve them.

### Background notes

- "The removal of the outer garment and the wrapping of a towel round the waist was the dress of menial service and would have been despised by both Jew and Greek alike... humility was despised in the ancient world as a sign of weakness. Jesus' command was therefore revolutionary in the sphere of human relationships" (New Bible Commentary).

# WEEK 9: DESTINY

*1 Corinthians 15:12-28*

[12] Now if Christ is proclaimed as raised from the dead, how can some of you say that there is no resurrection of the dead? [13] But if there is no resurrection of the dead, then not even Christ has been raised. [14] And if Christ has not been raised, then our preaching is in vain and your faith is in vain. [15] We are even found to be misrepresenting God, because we testified about God that he raised Christ, whom he did not raise if it is true that the dead are not raised. [16] For if the dead are not raised, not even Christ has been raised. [17] And if Christ has not been raised, your faith is futile and you are still in your sins. [18] Then those also who have fallen asleep in Christ have perished. [19] If in Christ we have hope in this life only, we are of all people most to be pitied.
[20] But in fact Christ has been raised from the dead, the firstfruits of those who have fallen asleep. [21] For as by a man came death, by a man has come also the resurrection of the dead. [22] For as in Adam all die, so also in Christ shall all be made alive. [23] But each in his own order: Christ the firstfruits, then at his coming those who belong to Christ. [24] Then comes the end, when he delivers the kingdom to God the Father after destroying every rule and every authority and power. [25] For he must reign until he has put all his enemies under his feet. [26] The last enemy to be destroyed is death. [27] For "God has put all things in subjection under his feet." But when it says, "all things are put in subjection," it is plain that he is excepted who put all things in subjection under him. [28] When all things are subjected to him, then the Son himself will also be subjected to him who put all things in subjection under him, that God may be all in all.

## Study Questions for 1 Corinthians 15:12-28

*Begin your study with a moment of prayer.*
*Ask God to open your heart and mind as you study his word.*

1. If the resurrection of Jesus never happened, what difference would it make in your life?

2. In this passage, Paul repeatedly contrasts the implications of the resurrection of Jesus with the implications of its denial. List the contrasts.

| Jesus is raised | Jesus is not raised |
|---|---|
|  |  |
|  |  |
|  |  |
|  |  |
|  |  |
|  |  |

3. Paul teaches that "the last enemy to be destroyed is death." How does this make you feel?

4. Paul states that we are to be in subjection under Christ (verse 27). What areas of your life need to be surrendered to Christ?

5. Write a prayer of thanks for the hope that God has given you.

# Next Steps: Additional Resources

In this section, you will find resources on the five main themes of the *Everyday Questions* study: the four fundamental worldview questions of origin, meaning, morality, and destiny, as well as the respectful, winsome approach modeled by Jonathan and Erica.

In the weekly study guide, each session is focused on a handful of key ideas. In this appendix, we have transitioned into providing resources that will offer you a broader overview. Now that you have become more familiar with these concepts and have practiced incorporating them into conversations with family and friends, you are ready to take the next step!

If the weekly study guide has offered some easy-to-follow directions for how to get from one place to another, this section is an introduction for how to navigate to anywhere you might want to go. We want to give you a practical roadmap for understanding what Christianity is all about and why it is a true and hopeful message.

To look at it another way, we can only share something with others if we already possess it ourselves. So if we are going to share our faith, it is essential that we are continuing to grow in our relationship with God, our understanding of the Scriptures, and our appreciation of the gospel. We will gain an ever-increasing confidence to share our faith as we become more prepared to ask great questions, respond to our friends' objections to Christianity, and explain why the Christian worldview is the most reasonable approach to life. And we will be encouraged to continue on this journey if we do it with a community of fellow believers who share our passion to love God and love our neighbors.

Our spiritually curious friends are not likely to come to Christ because we know all the answers or are theological black belts. Rather, their interest in Jesus is most likely to increase as we pray for them and love them. In the context of trust and respect, we can best raise questions that open our friends up to considering a new perspective on life. As they become increasingly interested in Jesus, we can serve them well by providing meaningful explanations for why Jesus can be trusted and followed. By demonstrating a complete dedication to Christ in our lives, we will become more authentic and trustworthy representatives of his message with our family and friends.

As you will see below, the remainder of the Next Steps study guide is arranged into five sections (Origin, Meaning, Morality, Destiny, and Relationships). Each section provides recommended Bible passages, articles, videos, and books.

Finally, we recommend you register for the RZIM Academy. This is a 12-week online course covering the topic of worldview, with a particular emphasis on the importance of engaging with individuals of different belief systems, and doing so with gentleness and respect. The course includes interaction with other students from around the world. A highly trained RZIM Academy moderator is on hand to facilitate the discussions and assist you with any questions. You can learn more at rzimacademy.org.

> *4 I thank my God always when I remember you in my prayers, 5 because I hear of your love and of the faith that you have toward the Lord Jesus and for all the saints, 6 and I pray that the sharing of your faith may become effective for the full knowledge of every good thing that is in us for the sake of Christ. 7 For I have derived much joy and comfort from your love, my brother, because the hearts of the saints have been refreshed through you.*
> —*Philemon 4-7*

# Next Steps: Origin

## Bible verses:

Genesis 1-3
Psalm 22:9-10
Psalm 90
Psalm 139:13-16
Isaiah 40:25-31
Matthew 6:25-34
John 1:1-5
Colossians 1:15-20
Revelation 4:9-11

## Articles:

"Windows Of Other Worlds" by Jill Carattini
    http://rzim.org/just-thinking/windows-of-other-worlds
"So Much More" by Danielle DuRant
    http://rzim.org/a-slice-of-infinity/so-much-more
"From Wonder to Understanding: Beginning a Journey" by Alister E. McGrath
    http://rzim.org/just-thinking/from-wonder-to-understanding-beginning-a-journey
"Think Again" by Ravi Zacharias
    http://rzim.org/just-thinking/think-again-deep-questions

## Videos:

Genesis: Made In God's Image by Simon Edwards
    https://www.youtube.com/watch?v=_6Oaw8H6gxI
Has Science Buried God? by John Lennox
    https://www.youtube.com/watch?v=PSq4KLjMSlI

Seven Days That Divide the World by John Lennox
   https://www.youtube.com/watch?v=0FmO2XKMe6g
What Does It Mean To Be Human? By Ravi Zacharias
   https://www.youtube.com/watch?v=1L29fPO4m6Q

## *Books:*

William Lane Craig and Quentin Smith, ***Theism, Atheism, and Big Bang Cosmology***
William A. Dembski, ed., ***Mere Creation: Science, Faith and Intelligent Design***
Norman L. Geisler and Frank Turek, ***I Don't Have Enough Faith To Be An Atheist***
Colin E. Gunton, ***Father, Son, and Holy Spirit: Toward a Fully Trinitarian Theology***
Phillip E. Johnson, ***The Wedge of Truth: Splitting The Foundations of Naturalism***
Phillip E. Johnson, ***Reason In The Balance: The Case Against Naturalism In Science, Law, And Education***
John C. Lennox, ***Gunning For God: Why The New Atheists Are Missing The Target***
Alister E. McGrath, ***The Twilight Of Atheism: The Rise And Fall Of Disbelief In The Modern World***
James Porter Moreland and John Mark Reynolds, eds., ***Three Views on Creation and Evolution***
Thomas Nagel, ***Mind And Cosmos: Why The Materialist Neo-Darwinian Conception Of Nature Is Almost Certainly False***
Alvin Plantinga, ***Where The Conflict Really Lies: Science, Religion, and Naturalism***
Michael Reeves, ***Delighting in the Trinity***
Gerald L. Schroeder, ***Genesis And The Big Bang: The Discovery Of Harmony Between Modern Science And The Bible***
Ravi Zacharias, ***The End Of Reason: A Response To The New Atheists***

# Next Steps: Meaning

## *Bible verses:*

Psalm 1
Psalm 112
Ecclesiastes
Matthew 6:25-34
Mark 12:28-34
John 6:35-40
John 8:12
Ephesians 2:1-10
Colossians 3:12-17
2 Timothy 4:1-5

## *Articles:*

"The Beginning of Words" by Jill Carattini
    http://rzim.org/a-slice-of-infinity/the-beginning-of-words
"Bread in Hand" by Jill Carattini
    http://rzim.org/a-slice-of-infinity/bread-in-hand
"The Essence of Life" by Stuart McAllister
    http://rzim.org/just-thinking/the-essence-of-life
"In Pursuit of Happiness" by Tejdor Tiewsoh
    http://rzim.org/a-slice-of-infinity/in-pursuit-of-happiness
"The Most Difficult Questions" by Ravi Zacharias
    http://rzim.org/a-slice-of-infinity/the-most-difficult-questions

## Videos:

God or No God? The Quest for Absolute Meaning by Ravi Zacharias
   https://www.youtube.com/watch?v=d_GJX4kQRd8
Need God? What If I Don't? by Ravi Zacharias
   https://www.youtube.com/watch?v=4lB0ucz3Gjc
The Problem of Pleasure by Ravi Zacharias
   https://www.youtube.com/watch?v=cu-ZbnowHUI
What Is Worthwhile Under the Sun? by Ravi Zacharias
   https://www.youtube.com/watch?v=1GTsIa8RJdo

## Books:

Os Guinness, *The Call: Finding And Fulfilling The Central Purpose Of Your Life*
C. S. Lewis, *The Weight of Glory*
Thomas V. Morris, *Making Sense of It All: Pascal and the Meaning of Life*
Paul K. Moser, *Why Isn't God More Obvious? – Finding the God Who Hides and Seeks*
Ravi Zacharias, *Can Man Live Without God?*
Ravi Zacharias, *Cries of The Heart: Bringing God Near When He Feels So Far*

# Next Steps: Morality

## Bible verses:

Exodus 20:1-17
Isaiah 51:1-8
Mark 7:14-23
Mark 12:28-34
Galatians 5:13-26
1 Peter 1:13-25

## Articles:

"Image and Ill-Repute" by Jill Carattini
    http://rzim.org/a-slice-of-infinity/image-and-ill-repute
"In Stone and Sand" by Jill Carattini
    http://rzim.org/a-slice-of-infinity/in-stone-and-sand
"Must the Moral Law Have A Moral Law-Giver?" by John Njoroge
    http://rzim.org/just-thinking/must-the-moral-law-have-a-lawgiver
"The New Atheism" by John Njoroge
    http://rzim.org/a-slice-of-infinity/the-new-atheism
"Nonsense or New Life?" by Ravi Zacharias
    http://rzim.org/a-slice-of-infinity/nonsense-or-new-life

## Videos:

Can We Be Good Without God? by Tanya Walker
    https://www.youtube.com/watch?v=mIqvU6cLj78
How Can a Good God Allow Evil? Does Life Have Meaning? by Ravi Zacharias
    https://www.youtube.com/watch?v=it7mhQ8fEq0
The Question of Suffering and the Goodness of God by Ravi Zacharias
    https://www.youtube.com/watch?v=jpjwM7Wz6Yk

## Books:

Henri Blocher, *Evil and The Cross: An Analytical Look at the Problem of Pain*
R. Douglas Geivett, *Evil and The Evidence For God*
Daniel Howard-Snyder, ed., *The Evidential Argument From Evil*
Peter Kreeft, *Making Sense Out Of Suffering*
C.S. Lewis, *A Grief Observed*
C. S. Lewis, *The Abolition of Man*
C. S. Lewis, *The Problem of Pain*
Alvin Plantinga, *God, Freedom, and Evil*
Vince Vitale and Ravi Zacharias, *Why Suffering?: Finding Meaning and Comfort When Life Doesn't Make Sense*

# Next Steps: Destiny

## *Bible verses:*

Psalm 138
Isaiah 46:8-13
Matthew 7:13-27
Romans 8:26-39
Philippians 3:12-21
1 Thessalonians 5:1-11
2 Peter 1:1-11
Revelation 21:1-4

## *Articles:*

"Dark Riddles" by Jill Carattini
    http://ca.rzim.org/a-slice-of-infinity/dark-riddles
"Dust and Ashes" by Margaret Manning
    http://rzim.org/a-slice-of-infinity/dust-and-ashes
"Acknowledging Creatureliness" by Stuart McAllister
    http://rzim.org/a-slice-of-infinity/acknowledging-creatureliness
"The Last Enemy" by John Njoroge
    http://rzim.org/a-slice-of-infinity/the-last-enemy-2

## Videos:

The Death and Resurrection of Jesus Christ
   https://www.youtube.com/watch?v=jwiUsOTC7ms&index=3&list=PLamW4K9v1K-lnsgK_2_G3B542D42FHRjp
Christianity, a Failed Hope? by Ravi Zacharias
   https://www.youtube.com/watch?v=AyJUNwHrlj0

## Books:

John R. W. Stott, ***The Cross Of Christ***
Lee Strobel, ***The Case For Christ: A Journalist's Personal Investigation of the Evidence for Jesus*** (see especially "Part 3: Researching the Resurrection")
John Wenham, Easter Enigma: ***Are the Resurrection Accounts in Conflict?***
Michael J. Wilkins and J.P. Moreland, eds., ***Jesus Under Fire: Modern Scholarship Reinvents the Historical Jesus*** (see especially the chapter "Did Jesus Rise From The Dead?" by William Lane Craig)
N. T. Wright, ***Surprised By Hope: Rethinking Heaven, the Resurrection, and the Mission of the Church***
N. T. Wright, ***The Resurrection Of The Son Of God (Christian Origins And The Question Of God, Vol. 3)***

# Next Steps: Relationships:

## *Bible verses:*

Matthew 9:35-38
Matthew 28:18-20
Luke 6:27-38
John 4:1-42
Acts 1:6-8
Romans 10:5-17
Romans 12:1-21
1 Corinthians 9:16-23
1 Corinthians 13
Galatians 5:13-26
Philemon 1:6
1 John 4:7-21
1 Peter 3:1-17

## *Articles::*

"Love and Rules" by Nathan Betts
    http://rzim.org/a-slice-of-infinity/love-and-rules
"Questions of Answers" by Jill Carattini
    http://rzim.org/a-slice-of-infinity/questions-of-answers
"Wasteful Love" by Jill Carattini
    http://rzim.org/a-slice-of-infinity/wasteful-love-2
"Questions in the Boat" by Margaret Manning
    http://rzim.org/a-slice-of-infinity/questions-in-the-boat
"Starting With a Question" by Tom Price
    http://rzim.org/a-slice-of-infinity/starting-with-a-question
"Let My People Think: Answering Life's Questions"
by Ravi Zacharias
    http://rzim.org/a-slice-of-infinity/questions-of-answers

## Videos:

Life's Four Big Questions - Ravi Zacharias and Abdu Murray at the University of Kentucky
https://www.youtube.com/watch?v=IRPLhnjyaRw
The Personal Side of Apologetics by Ravi Zacharias and Stuart McAllister
https://www.youtube.com/watch?v=JTJo62YAl3M

## Books:

Paul Copan, ***When God Goes To Starbucks: A Guide to Everyday Apologetics***
Greg Koukl, ***Tactics***
Sean McDowell, ***Apologetics for a New Generation: A Biblical and Culturally Relevant Approach to Talking About God***
Alister McGrath, ***Mere Apologetics: How to Help Seekers and Skeptics Find Faith***
Randy Newman, ***Questioning Evangelism***
Rebecca Manley Pippert, ***Out of the Saltshaker and Into the World***
Rick Richardson, ***Reimagining Evangelism***
Ravi Zacharias and Norman Geisler, ***Is Your Church Ready? Motivating Leaders to Live an Apologetic Life***